Hanging Out with Jesus Again

'Only Bob Hartman could tell the story of Jesus with so many pants, bottoms and nostrils and get away with it. The gospel stories from the point of view of three disciples who have a distinctly childlike attitude to bodily functions, religious jargon and the mystery of faith. Huge fun.'

Lucy Moore, Messy Church

'The illustrations are brilliant and the storytelling just what you'd expect from somebody who has held generations of children spellbound.'

Rob Parsons OBE, Founder and Chairman, Care for the Family

'My daughter was laughing from the word "Pants" in chapter one – biblical brilliance from Bob once again! Compelling & hilarious!'

Tom Elliott, Comedian and Magician

'Bob's writing is just fabulous. The stories leap off the page. These tales of friends getting things wrong, puzzling it all out, is a great reminder that the disciples were really rather like us. Bob's skill at storytelling is

first class. Oh, and if you didn't know – these stories go back a long way! I bet you just didn't know how funny they could be. A fab book for your bookshelf, your eyes and your heart. Bob's done it again!'
Paul Kerensa, Comedian and Writer

'Bob Hartman has the knack of finding humour in any situation. His invitation to hang out with Jesus will capture the imagination of many children. As they laugh at the antics of Pip, Tommo and Bart they will also discover the love and teaching of Jesus.'
Mary Hawes, National Children & Youth Adviser

'Laugh out loud, feel good, family fun. I love it.'
Steve Legg, Magician

Hanging Out with Jesus Again

Bob Hartman

Illustrated by Mark Beech

Authentic

Text copyright © Bob Hartman 2021
Illustrations copyright © Mark Beech 2021

27 26 25 24 23 22 21 7 6 5 4 3 2 1

First published 2021 by Authentic Media Limited.
PO Box 6326, Bletchley, Milton Keynes, MK1 9GG.
authenticmedia.co.uk

The right of Bob Hartman to be identified as the Author of this Work has been asserted in accordance with the Copyright, Design and Patents Act 1988.

All rights reserved.
No part of this publication may be reproduced, stored in a retrieval system, or transmitted in any form or by any means, electronic, mechanical, photocopying, recording or otherwise, without prior permission of the publisher or a licence permitting restricted copying.
In the UK such licences are issued by the Copyright Licensing Agency, 5th Floor, Shackleton House, 4 Battle Bridge Lane, London SE1 2HX.

British Library Cataloguing in Publication Data
A catalogue record for this book is available from the British Library.

ISBN 978-1-78893-119-9
978-1-78893-120-5 (e-book)

Cover design by Mark Beech

Printed and bound by CPI Group (UK) Ltd,
Croydon, CR0 4YY.

For Leah. Big Bart's Biggest Fan.

Contents

Chapter 1	**PANTS**	1
Chapter 2	**LEOPARDS**	13
Chapter 3	**QUEUE**	25
Chapter 4	**COAT**	37
Chapter 5	**RHYME**	49
Chapter 6	**HANDS**	61
Chapter 7	**DONKEY**	73
Chapter 8	**TEMPLE**	89
Chapter 9	**WIDOW**	101
Chapter 10	**NARD**	113
Chapter 11	**HANKIE**	127
Chapter 12	**GHOST**	143

Chapter 1

PANTS

"It's obvious isn't it?"

*I*t was the Sabbath Day. We had nearly reached the synagogue. As usual, Bart and Tommo and I were following a little way behind Jesus and the other disciples.

"I hope it's not boring," Bart sighed. "I hate it when the synagogue services are boring."

"Jesus is giving the talk," said Tommo. "It'll be great!"

"No, I mean the other bits," Bart sighed again. "The singey, prayey, readey bits."

"No need to worry there, either, my large friend," I assured him, "at least as far as the singing goes. This is one of those modern, fancy, new-fangled synagogues."

"Whadda you mean?" grunted Tommo.

"Well, for a start," I explained, "there's more than one instrument. Not just a harp, not just a lyre, not just a cymbal, but a whole band!"

"Very Psalm 150!" Bart grinned.

"Exactly!" I replied. "Trumpets, tambourines, they've got the lot. And dancers, too! What's more, you don't even have to know the words to the psalms."

"What?" Tommo grunted again.

"No, they hang these huge scrolls at the front, between two ladders. And there are helpers who climb the ladders and turn the scrolls when the psalms change."

"That must be tricky," said Tommo.

"They fall behind every now and then," I agreed. "But who can blame them? It works most of the time."

"I hope they have a scroll for my favourite synagogue song," said Bart.

"I did not know you had a favourite synagogue song," I replied.

"OH YES," Bart nodded vigorously. "It has been my favourite since I was a little-boy-Bart. It is based on Psalm 42."

Tommo scratched his head. "Not familiar with that one, Big Fella."

"That's why you need a hanging-at-the-front giant scroll," I chuckled.

Then Bart chuckled, too, and said, "As the Deer Pants. Heh-heh. That's my **favourite** psalm."

"And why would that be, exactly?" Tommo inquired.

"Deer. Pants. It's obvious, isn't it?" Bart chuckled again. "And it's hilarious! Do they wear boxers? Do they wear briefs? Is there some sort of special springy deer underwear? I do not know. But I find the whole idea strangely compelling."

"Yeah," Tommo muttered, "And some of us just find you strange—"

I cleared my throat. "Actually," I interrupted, "the psalm isn't about that. You need to read the rest of the line: "As the deer pants for the water."

"I see," Bart slowly nodded. "Deer pants for the water? It's about swimming trunks, then! I stand corrected!"

I just sighed. "No, it's got nothing to do with what deer wear on their bottoms. Deer don't wear anything on their bottoms! It's not about those kind of pants at all. It's about what you do when you're thirsty." And then I made a little doggy, deery, panting sound to show him what I meant.

Bart nodded again. "It's all becoming clear to me now," he said. "It's not a deer. It's a donkey."

"A what?" grunted Tommo.

"A donkey," Bart repeated. "Like the one over there. Panting."

Tommo and I turned around, and sure enough, there was a donkey tied up to a post. And, yes, it was panting away, desperate for a drink.

"As the donkey pants for the water," Bart sang slowly.

But before he could finish his song, a man in some very fine robes appeared.

"I'm terribly sorry, Turnip," the man said to the donkey. "I was so **busy** preparing for the service that I forgot all about you. You must be parched!" Then he untied the donkey and led her to a trough nearby. "That's a good girl," he muttered, patting her on the back. "Drink as much as you like."

"Aww," said Bart, rubbing a little tear from his eye. "He really loves that donkey, doesn't he? He needs to buy her a nice pair of pants."

Tommo looked at me as if to say, "It's not worth it."

Then Jesus called: "You boys ready? It's about time for the synagogue service to start."

So in we went. And wouldn't you know it, the very first song to appear on the giant hanging scrolls at the front was . . .

"As the deer pants!" shouted Bart. And then he turned to me with a worried look on his face. "Do you think we should tell them, Pip?" he asked. "Tell them that it should be 'donkey' instead of 'deer'?"

"We'll tell them afterwards," I whispered. "Just sing."

So Bart did. And so did I. Sang with all our hearts. And then Tommo turned to me, too. "How long are we gonna sing this thing?" he grunted. "We've done it, like, thirty-seven times, by my count."

"The words are meant to soak in," I whispered back.

"Well, I'm drowning," Tommo moaned. "And what's with the guy on the tambourine? Do they let just anybody play those things?"

"It's not the art, it's what's in your heart," I replied. "It's about getting close to God."

Then Bart raised a finger in the air. "As the donkey pants for the water, so my soul longs after you."

"Yes, exactly!" I nodded. "Well, sort of . . ." And then, mercifully, the song finished. And Jesus walked to the front and sat down to teach.

"I have a story for you," he began. "My dad was a carpenter . . ."

I loved it when Jesus told stories. And I was looking forward to hearing what he had to say. Bart, however, was still singing quietly to himself.

"**Shhhh!**" I shushed him.

"But it has a ring to it, don't you think?" he whispered back. "As the donkey pants for the water."

Fortunately, I don't think Jesus could hear him.

"I learned a lot from my dad," Jesus went on. "Sawing, **hammering**, piecing together. But the thing I loved most was the polishing. And he would be right there at my side, encouraging me. 'Rub away,' he would say. 'Make it shine, Jesus, shine!'"

Bart just grinned. "Shine, Jesus, shine," he chuckled. "That has a ring to it, too!"

And then Jesus stopped talking. Not because of anything Bart said, but because he had seen something. Someone, rather. A woman in the crowd who could not stand up straight.

"Come over here," he called to her. And she went, back bent, eyes facing the floor.

"For eighteen years," she explained, "some evil spirit has bound me and made me like this."

"Well, you are free now," said Jesus. And when he laid his hand on her back, she stood up straight, tears running down her face.

"Praise God!" she shouted. "Praise God, I'm healed!"

"I think that's our cue to sing again!" Bart beamed.

"I think you should just shut up and enjoy the moment," whispered Tommo, annoyed.

Turns out he wasn't the only one. The man in charge of the synagogue looked pretty annoyed, as well. He stood and faced the crowd and said,

"There are six whole days in every week when we can do work, like making people well. If you want to be healed, come on one of those days, not on the Sabbath when we are meant to rest from work!"

The woman who had been healed looked confused. She looked like she thought she had done something wrong. She looked like she was going to cry. And that's when Bart stood up.

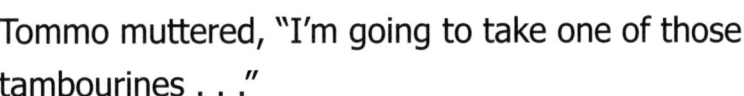

"If he starts singing that song again," Tommo muttered, "I'm going to take one of those tambourines . . ."

But Bart didn't start singing. No. He pointed his finger in the direction of the man in charge of the synagogue and shouted,

"Now hang on, just a minute, Mister Donkey Pants—"

Every face in the synagogue turned Bart's way.

Whether it was because he had spoken out or because he had addressed the ruler of the synagogue by a name no one had ever heard before, or was likely to hear again, I do not know. But he definitely had everyone's attention.

"I was outside the synagogue with my friends," Bart began, "waiting for the service to start. Your donkey was panting, wasn't she? She was thirsty. So you untied her and led her to a water trough to have a drink. I thought you were a **very** nice man to do that, Mister Donkey Pants. But I'm not so sure now."

"Because that was a kind of work, wasn't it?" Jesus interrupted, looking at the ruler of the synagogue. "The kind of work our law allows. Work you did because you care for your donkey. So, if it's all right for you to do that kind of work to free your donkey and lead it to water, what is **wrong** with the work I did to free this woman from the bonds of the devil that bent her back and bound her all these years?"

The ruler of the synagogue had no answer for that. He knew that Jesus was right, and he looked at his feet, ashamed. And everyone else in the synagogue? They raised their voices, praising God for the AMAZING thing that had happened to the woman.

And Bart raised his voice, too.

"Here it comes," Tommo sighed. "Another thirty-seven verses."

And so it did, in a **toe-tapping**, tambourine-shaking, giant-scroll-at-the-front-hanging, Big-Bart song of praise:

"As the donkey pants for the water, so my soul longs after you!"

Chapter 2

LEOPARDS

"Following Jesus has definitely had its share of surprises."

"Aaaa-choo!" I sneezed. And then I sneezed "Aaa-choo!" again.

"Still got that cold, haven't you?" grunted Tommo.

"Yeah," I sniffled. "Doesn't seem to want to go away."

"That is because you have consistently refused to use my Aunt Susanna's Guaranteed-to-Never-Fail Cold and Sneezing Remedy," said Bart.

"And that is because you have consistently refused to tell me what is IN your Aunt Susanna's

Guaranteed-to-Never-Fail Cold and Sneezing Remedy!" I replied.

And then I sneezed again.

"How many times do I have to tell you?" Bart snapped back. "It is a secret recipe that I have promised never to reveal, even to my very best friends."

"But as your very best friends," Tommo said, "your ONLY friends, in fact, as far as I can tell, we have heard enough stories about your strange relatives to assume that this so-called remedy contains at least one ingredient that is absolutely **disgusting**. Have you forgotten the mudbeard you made me?"

"I have not," Bart said proudly. "It was a lovely mudbeard as I recall. Perfectly shaped. Finely fashioned. You got a date out of it, if memory serves."

"Yes, who dumped me the minute it cracked and fell off my face and she discovered the bits of straw and poo that were **hidden** in it!" Tommo shouted.

"Somebody is very grumpy today," Bart noted.

"No, somebody – well, both of us somebodies – are just **suspicious**," I said.

"All right, then," Bart sighed. "I will tell you what is in my Aunt Susanna's Guaranteed-to-Never-Fail Cold and Sneezing Remedy if you promise not to breathe a word of it to another soul."

"Promise," I promised.

But Tommo was suddenly distracted. "Something's going on, up ahead," he said. "With Jesus and the other disciples. I'll go check it out 'cos I don't actually care what's in your dopey aunt's dopey medicine."

"More grumpy than usual," Bart whispered.

"Yeah. So what's in it?" I asked.

"Well, there is a lot of milk, for a start," Bart began. "Cow milk. Goat milk. Sheep milk."

"Lots of dairy." I nodded, "Sounds all right, so far."

"And then there is fat," Bart went on. "Cow fat. Goat fat. Sheep fat."

"Getting a little **queasy** now," I admitted.

"It's all mixed in," said Bart. "The congealed stuff that you scrape off meat. You'd hardly know it was there."

"Anything else?" I asked.

"Just a few random things, really," Bart replied. "A bit of bladder."

I gagged.

"A slice of spleen."

I gagged again.

"A couple of colons."

I put my hand over my mouth.

"A hint of intestine."

My gut was churning now.

"And a spoonful of partially digested cud, scraped from the inside of a cow's stomach."

And that's when the contents of MY stomach appeared, spraying across the grass and the path and my sandals.

"That is the most disgusting thing I have ever heard!" I gulped. "I will never, ever, ever drink your Aunt Susanna's Guaranteed-to-Never-Fail Cold and Sneezing Remedy!"

"But it's working already!" Bart exclaimed. "You

haven't sneezed once since I started telling you what's in it!"

"That's because it made me . . . oh, never mind!" I sighed.

And that's when Tommo reappeared. "I found out what the problem is," he reported. "There are lepers ahead. Ten of them."

"Oh dear," Bart said. "They are very dangerous."

"Not if you stay away from them," I replied.

"But they look very scary," Bart trembled. "All covered with spots."

"Well, yeah, some of them have different coloured patches of skin, I suppose," said Tommo.

"And the claws!" Bart continued. "The nasty, sharp claws!"

"Hang on," I said, holding up my hand. "Are we talking about the same thing here? Because the last time I checked, lepers do not have nasty, sharp claws. In fact, the disease they have is so terrible that sometimes their fingers actually fall off. So what are you talking about Bart?"

"Leopards," Bart muttered. "I thought Tommo said 'leopards'". Then he paused for a moment before speaking again. "Can I point out, though, that it was an honest mistake. As I understand it, it is no longer appropriate to refer to people by their illness. So instead of calling them 'lepers', we should be calling them 'people with leprosy'. If Tommo had simply done that, I would not have confused ten people who have a deadly disease, that's catching, with a spotted African carnivore."

Tommo sighed. "So now it's my fault that you can't tell the difference between 'leper' and 'leopard'?"

"People with **leprosy**!" Bart insisted. "I mean, how would you like it if we identified you by what was wrong with you? What if we called poor Pip, here, Sneezy? What if we called you Grumpy?"

"What if we called you dopey?" Tommo added. "It would fit, that's what!"

"It would make you a very small person," Bart replied. "And I think you're bigger than that."

"Look," I sighed, "why don't we just go and see what's going on with these ten . . . people with leprosy?"

The people with leprosy were keeping a safe distance. That was good. And they wanted Jesus to help them.

"Jesus! Master! Show us your mercy!" they shouted.

So Jesus said to them, "Go! Find a priest and show yourselves to him." And they went.

Bart was, of course, confused, yet again. "I don't get it," he shrugged. "Why did Jesus send them to see a priest? Why didn't he heal them?"

"I think he did," I said. "I mean, we're not close enough to tell, are we? They stayed away so we wouldn't catch what they have. That's what they're supposed to do. But if they get healed of their leprosy, then they are allowed to get close to other people again. And it's up to a priest to inspect them and make that decision. I think that's why Jesus sent them away."

And just then, one of them returned.

"Thank you, thank you, thank you, Jesus!" he shouted. "The leprosy is gone! Praise God!" And he threw himself at Jesus' feet.

"Hang on," Tommo muttered. "That accent. It's strange. That man's not Jewish like us. He's a . . . Samaritan!"

Bart rolled his eyes.

"There you go again. Putting people into little boxes. Sneezy, Grumpy, Dopey, Leper. And now Samaritan. This is Not making me very happy!"

"But Samaritans are our enemies!" Tommo protested. "And have been for centuries. They married the people that **destroyed** our land. They worship God differently. They're foreigners! What's Jesus doing healing one of them?"

"Because he needed help?" I muttered.

Then Jesus himself turned to address us.

"I healed ten people, didn't I?" he said. "Where are the other nine? That's what I want to know. It seems that it is only this 'foreigner' who has taken the time to come back and give thanks to God."

Then he looked at the Samaritan and smiled. "Stand up," Jesus told the man. "Stand up and go. You **trusted** me. And because of that you are healed."

"See, Tommo," said Bart. "Jesus doesn't care what a person is called or where they come from. He's just happy when they trust him."

Tommo grunted and looked at the ground and mumbled something.

"**C'mon**," Bart said. "If you have something to say, Tommo, spit it out. Don't be Bashful."

"I don't know," Tommo sighed. "Maybe it's just that Jesus keeps doing things I don't expect him to do. Like **helping** people who aren't like us – even people who are our **enemies**. I know we all think that he's the you-know-what – the Messiah – but sometimes what he does makes me wonder, that's all."

"I think that's a good thing," Bart grinned. "How boring would it be if everything was just like we expected it to be?"

I nodded. "Following Jesus has definitely had its share of surprises."

"Yeah, well, I'm not much of a fan of surprises," Tommo grunted.

"Then you definitely don't want to know what's in my Aunt Susanna's Guaranteed-to-Never-Fail Cold and Sneezing Remedy," said Bart.

Then he turned to me and whispered, "Don't tell him about the undigested cow cud, Pip."

And I vomited again, of course. No surprises there.

Chapter 3

QUEUE

"Found a nostril!"

"*I* hate queues!" Tommo grumbled. "I flippin' hate queues!"

"But I love goat-on-a-stick!" was all Bart could say in reply. "Chewy and gooey goat down your throaty! What could be better?"

"Catching up with the others!" Tommo grunted. "If we hadn't stopped for your stupid snack, we never would have fallen behind, in the first place. This queue would not have appeared out of nowhere, in the second place. And we would be where we're supposed to be, in the third place. NOT STUCK IN SOME FLIPPIN' QUEUE!"

"Well there must be a reason," I suggested. It was, of course, exactly the wrong thing to suggest.

"Reason? Reason!" Tommo moaned. "There is never 'reason' where queues are concerned. Someone will be repairing the road. That's what they'll tell you. But when you get there, there will be shovels and picks **scattered** about, but no one will be working. No one at all!"

"I found a bit of hoof." Bart grinned, "YUM!"

"Or there will be leaves on the road," Tommo continued as if Bart had never spoken at all. "The wrong kind of leaves, of course. Leaves that slow everything down to a crawl!"

"And, look," Bart exclaimed. "Here is a chewy chunk of horn!"

"Or, worst of all, and even more infuriating," Tommo ranted on. "There will be **nothing**! That's right! No accident. No incident. No clue whatsoever as to why you've just wasted twenty minutes of your life, waiting in a flippin' queue!"

"Found a nostril!" Bart shouted, plucking it out with one finger. "Look! I'm picking a goat's nose." Then he popped it in his mouth. "Hmm," he noted. "There's something sweet and gooey inside . . ."

"Will you just shut up about that goat and help me figure out what's going on here!" Tommo shouted.

"Give me a minute," Bart replied, holding a sticky finger in the air. "I am almost finished. And once I am finished, I need time to savour the experience, to reflect on every last bit of goaty goodness that has passed between my lips."

"I'll help you, Tommo," I said. "I suspect that Bart could be occupied with that for quite a while."

"I don't get it," Tommo moaned, surveying the crowd. "There are loads of people here. And most of them are kids! What could they possibly be waiting for? Maybe we should just push past."

Now it was my turn to raise a finger in the air. "I'm terribly sorry," I said. "But I simply cannot do that."

"And why not?" asked Tommo.

"Because it would violate one of my most deeply held beliefs – the sacredness of the queue."

Tommo rolled his eyes.

"Hear me out," I went on. "You may hate queues, Tommo. And we have heard your reasons. But I'm afraid that I take the opposite view. For I am convinced that the humble queue is all that stands between us and chaos. It is what separates us from the barbarians."

"**Barbarians**?" said Bart, licking his fingers and joining the conversation. "I could seriously use a haircut, so if there's a barbarian nearby—"

"Not a barber!" Tommo interrupted. "A **barbarian**! You know, a raging, wild-eyed, maniacal person with a huge sharp sword."

"Sounds exactly like my barber," Bart replied.

"Barbers? Barbarians? What does it matter?" I shouted. "All I know is that if we jump this queue, someone will follow, then someone else will follow them, and every bit of order will come crashing down around us!"

"What order?" Tommo shrugged. "There are kids running **everywhere**. Their parents are chasing after them. This isn't a queue. It's a crowd. It's a mob."

"But there is always hope," I replied. "If we stand calmly and wait our turn, others will join us, trust me. I am convinced that there is a race of people, somewhere, who share my passion and are just longing to join a queue, whatever the reason, whatever the season, whatever the time. People living in some wonderful, orderly . . . Waitingland."

"Sounds more like Crazyland to me," Tommo muttered.

Then something hit Bart on the head. Something round and brown and smelly. But Bart was not bothered, not one bit.

"Splodgeball!" he shouted. "The kids are playing splodgeball!" Then he reached down and picked up a pile of poo and formed a round, brown, smelly ball of his own. And chucked it into the crowd. "Just missed!" he called to some child who had managed to duck out of the way. Followed, shortly, by a "Sorry, madam!"

Tommo just shook his head. "Why is it that, everywhere we go, somebody is always doing something with poo? Or farting? Or puking? Or picking their nose?"

"It was a goat's nose, to be clear," Bart corrected him. "And why not? **Splodgeball** is fun! I played it all the time when I was an itty-bitty Bart."

"And the point is?" Tommo sighed.

"I would have thought that was **obvious**," Bart replied, "To be splodged as much as possible. You set a time, you throw your splodgeballs, and the one who has the most splodge on his clothes at the end is the winner."

"Are you sure about that?" asked Tommo.

"**Of course**!" Bart grinned. "I used to win all the time. At least that's what the other boys told me."

"So you basically just throw poo at each other?" I said.

"It's much more complicated than that," Bart replied. "In fact, it's an art! If the poo has been deposited recently on the ground, it will be too wet and slip right through your fingers. But if it has sat there for a while and baked in the sun, it will be too hard to shape into a splodgeball. Ideally, it needs to have rested there just long enough to get crusty on the outside whilst retaining a soft pliable center. Like this one, in fact . . ."

Then Bart bent down and made another **splodgeball** before running off into the crowd.

"So would you call that 'jumping the queue'?" Tommo grunted.

"I don't even begin to know what I'd call it," I said. "But I suspect Bart is going to be gone for a very long time."

"And I suspect he's going to be covered all over in splodge when he returns," Tommo noted. "He's a BIG target!"

And that's when we heard a BIG voice.

"Listen up, everybody!" The voice called out across the crowd. "I know that you are here to see Jesus, but I have to tell you that he is very busy today."

"Hang on!" Tommo grumbled in my direction.

"I recognise that voice. It's Peter! You mean to tell me that these people are here to see Jesus? That's what this queue is for?"

"Looks like it," I muttered. "So I guess it wouldn't, strictly speaking, be jumping the queue if we joined the others up front."

"Seeing as that's where we're supposed to be in the first place!" Tommo groaned. "Let's go!"

So off we went, excusing ourselves here, apologising there, explaining who we were to everyone along the way.

"We only want Jesus to bless our children!" one woman said.

"It won't take long," said another one.

"We've been waiting for ages!" added a man who sounded just like Tommo.

We couldn't promise anything, of course. We didn't know what was going on at the front of the queue. Until we got there, at least.

And then we understood. There were sick people, loads of them, waiting to be healed. Jesus was doing his best, but they just kept coming. That's when Peter addressed the crowd once again. "You're going to have to take these children home," he shouted. "Jesus is healing the sick. He has more important things to do than pray for your kids!"

"Flippin' fisherman," Tommo muttered.

But someone else was not so quiet. And that someone else was Jesus! "Hang on!" he said, looking straight at Peter. And it was a not-very-happy look.

"Don't keep these children away from me!" Jesus insisted. "I want them near me. The kingdom of heaven is made up of people who see the world just like they do."

Peter opened his mouth to reply, but before he could say a word, a splodgeball came hurtling through the air and hit him square on the chest. He looked down, disgusted, as Bart and a whole gang of children emerged from the crowd, each and every one of them covered with poo. And Bart, of course, was the pooiest of them all.

Jesus looked at Bart and smiled. "In fact," he continued, "if you're ever going to understand the kingdom, you're going to have to enter it like a child. Trusting. Innocent. Open hearted."

Then Jesus sat down and motioned for the parents and their children to come forward. And, one by one, he blessed them.

"I won!" Bart grinned, pointing at his shirt. "And Jesus knows it too! Did you see the way he smiled at me?"

"I did," I grinned back. "Well done, Big Fella. In more ways than one." And then I paused and looked at the crowd. "But I have to go." I said. "There is a **very** important matter that needs attending to. And I am just the man to do it!"

Off I went to mingle amongst the parents and their children. "Form a **queue**, now," I insisted. "Take your turn. No jumping out of line. And that way everyone will get a chance to see Jesus."

I was in my element, at last. In that wonderful, orderly place called Waitingland.

Chapter 4

COAT

"Purple, that's the giveaway."

We were just hanging out – me, Tommo, Bart, Jesus, and the rest of the crew, of course – when we saw this guy walking in our direction.

"Nice coat," observed Tommo. "Expensive."

"How do you know?" I asked.

"Had a lot of rich clients when I was doing that catering job," he replied. "Purple, that's the giveaway."

"I had a nice coat once," Bart mused.

"Not as nice as that one," Tommo assured him.

"Oh, much nicer," Bart replied. "My Uncle Jacob made it for me. It had loads of different colours.

Reds and greens and yellows and blues. And, yes, purples. I was his favourite, you see."

"Your Uncle Jacob?" Tommo grunted.

"A coat of *many* colours?" I added. "You aren't confusing your story with the story of Joseph, by any chance, are you?"

"I don't know anybody called Joseph," Bart shrugged.

"Nobody is saying that you do," said Tommo. "It's a story from the Book of the Law. You know, Joseph and his jealous brothers?"

Bart shook his head. "Sorry. Doesn't ring a bell. Now that you mention it, though, my brothers were very *jealous* of me. And my coat. And my dreams, of course."

"Bart!" I said, "That is exactly what happens in the story of Joseph!"

"So this Joseph had dreams, too?" asked Bart.

"Yes," I replied.

"And they made his brothers angry?"

"Yes," said Tommo.

"And did his dreams come true?"

"Yes," we answered together.

"So he ended up running his own goat-on-a-stick stand?" Bart grinned.

"NO!" we moaned.

"Because that was my dream," said Bart. "See, I'm nothing like this Joseph person."

"Fair enough," I said. "Sorry I brought it up."

"And so you should be," said Bart. "It's a very **painful** memory. My brothers took my coat, smeared it with chicken blood and told my uncle Jacob that I had been eaten by a goat."

I looked at Tommo. "I'm **not** going there again," I sighed.

"Don't blame you," he sighed back.

That's when the rich man spoke. "Good teacher," he began, looking at Jesus. "What do I have to do to live for ever with God?"

"Good question," I whispered.

"Bet Jesus has a good answer," whispered Tommo, in reply.

But the answer wasn't what any of us expected. In fact, it was another question.

"Why do you call me 'Good'"? Jesus asked him. "You do realise that only God deserves to be called good?"

"But if Jesus is who we think he is . . ." Bart whispered, "who Peter said he is, then . . ."

"Yeah, yeah, we get it," Tommo whispered back.

"Well, you know the commandments," Jesus went on. "Don't commit adultery. Don't murder. Don't steal. Don't lie. Honour your father and mother."

"I do," the man replied, "and I have kept them all since I was a boy."

"Not like my brothers," Bart grumbled. "They murdered me and fed me to a goat."

"No, they didn't," I said, "otherwise you wouldn't be sitting here. But they **did** lie to your Uncle Jacob about it. I'll give you that."

Bart shook his head sadly, "And then they sold me into slavery."

"Who's lying now?" Tommo muttered.

"They did!" Bart insisted. "They **really** did! To a man with a toilet-scrubbing business. He worked me so hard I might as well have been a slave. I cleaned a potty here. A potty there. And a potty far, far away."

Tommo rolled his eyes. "And I suppose his wife fancied you?"

"Of course she did," Bart replied, proudly. "Her husband scrubbed toilets for a living. Is it any wonder that she preferred someone who dreamed of running his own **goat-on-a-stick** stand?"

Jesus, meanwhile, was considering the rich man's answer.

"There's just one thing you're missing," Jesus told him. "Sell everything you have. Give whatever money you make to the poor. Then you will have treasure in heaven. And when you have done that, come and follow me."

"What? EveryThing?" The man replied. "But you don't understand. I am wealthy. Extremely wealthy." And he looked as though he was about to cry.

Jesus sighed. "And that is why it is difficult — **extremely** difficult — for a wealthy man to enter the kingdom of God." And then Jesus smiled a little smile. "In fact," he said, "it's easier for a camel to squeeze its way through the eye of a needle than for a rich person to squeeze himself into the kingdom of God."

"That's funny," Bart chuckled. "Where does the camel start? With his camelly nose? With his camelly foot? With his camelly bottom?"

"I think the joke is that it's impossible, wherever he starts," I said.

"Which makes no sense!" grunted

Tommo. "I always thought that riches were a blessing from God, that making somebody wealthy was God's way of rewarding them for doing the right thing."

Then he put up his hand. "But Jesus," Tommo asked, "if a rich man has trouble getting into God's kingdom, then what hope do the rest of us have? How can anybody be saved?"

"Because anything is possible with God," Jesus replied.

That's when Peter put up his hand. "Well, we have given up a lot to follow you," he said. "We've left our homes and our families behind."

"Flippin' fisherman," Tommo whispered. "Always trying to score points."

But Jesus liked what Peter said. "I mean this, I really do," said Jesus, "Anyone who has given up the home he loves or the family he loves for the sake of God's kingdom, will receive many times more than that, both now and in the age to come."

"Let me get this straight," Tommo whispered again, "God doesn't bless us when we 'get stuff', he blesses us when we 'give stuff away'? That doesn't make any sense."

"Sure it does," Bart grinned. "My whole life changed when I gave up my dream of running my own goat-on-a-stick stand."

"Let me guess," Tommo sighed. "You went to Egypt, you interpreted Pharaoh's dream, he put you in charge of storing up food and you saved everyone, including your brothers, from **starvation**?"

Bart stared at him blankly. "I have no idea what you are talking about."

"It's the rest of the story of Joseph," I explained. "But now that you mention it, Tommo, Joseph did have to lose a lot before his dream came true, didn't he?"

"Yeah, well, I guess he did," said Tommo. "He was nearly murdered by his brothers, for a start."

"Just like me," Bart noted.

"He became a slave."

"Just like me," Bart said again.

"He was thrown into prison."

"Just like me," Bart repeated.

"C'mon Bart," I sighed, "You were never thrown into prison."

"I was locked in a loo by that toilet-scrubbing man," Bart replied. "Does that count?"

"Was it prison?" asked Tommo.

"Not exactly," Bart answered, "but it was horrible. Someone had made the most enormous dump. And there were flies buzzing round it and horrible fumes rising from it and bits of undigested goat sticking out of it and . . ."

"Hang on," I said. "That dump didn't happen to come from you, by any chance, did it?"

Bart paused for moment. "As a matter of fact, it did!" he replied. "And I think the toilet-scrubbing man said something about staying in there till I had cleaned up every last bit."

"Leaving dumps behind . . ." I continued.

"Which is what one does with **dumps**," Bart noted.

"Leaving dumps behind," I sighed, "and returning to the story of Joseph, he did lose a lot along the way, which meant he had to turn to God for help, right?"

"He did," Tommo nodded.

"So maybe that's what Jesus means," I concluded. "Maybe what he's saying is that if we have lots of stuff, we depend on that, but when we let go of our stuff or lose it in some other way, then we have to turn to God. And that's when we get blessed!"

"That is **brilliant**, Pip!" Bart grinned. "And, as I said a little while ago, that is exactly what happened to me when I let go of my dreams for a goat-on-a-stick stand."

"That's what you let go of," said Tommo, "but I can't see that you got anything."

And that's when Big Bart put one big arm around Tommo and his other big arm around me. "I

got to hang out with you guys!" he beamed. "That's what. And Jesus and the others, too, of course. My best mates!"

Tommo went quiet, and I wiped a little something from my eye.

"Well that's very nice of you to say," I mumbled as I glanced at Tommo. "And I'm sure we . . . we . . . feel the same way."

"Of course you do!" Bart said. "You're just like brothers to me. Better, in fact, because I know that whatever happens . . ."

"We would always have your back," I said.

Bart shook his head. "No."

"We would never let you down?" suggested Tommo.

Bart shook his head again. "No, I would have thought it was obvious. I know that whatever happens, the two of you would NeVeR murder me and feed me to a goat!"

Chapter 5

RHYME

"Why are we eating with a man in a tree?"

We were on our way to Jerusalem. We had almost reached Jericho. Tommo was shuffling along. I was looking at the scenery. And for some strange reason, Bart was singing:

"We're going down to Jericho town.
We're going to have a look around.
My sandals and my hair are brown
And Tommo is wearing a grumpy frown.
Going down to Jericho town,
Going down to Jericho town,

Going down to Jericho town,
Going down to Jericho town."

Well, I say "singing", but it was actually a kind of rhyming singy thing. Not really a proper song at all. And he didn't do it just once. No, he kept doing it, over and over again.

Finally, Tommo **exploded**. "What in heaven's name are you doing?" he shouted.

Bart stopped. "Don't know, really," he said. "But I do know that I like it. It's fun. And it's catchy."

"It's **annoying**!" Tommo shouted again. "And you put my name in it!"

"Well, that's how it works," Bart shrugged.

"How what works?" I asked. "You don't even know what you're doing!"

"But I do know that it needs to rhyme, that you have to make up the rhyme as you go, and it has to be about something that is happening around you. Like Tommo with his grumpy face."

"I do NOT have a grumpy face!" said Tommo . . . grumpily. "This is how I always look."

"Yeah, grumpy," Bart replied.

"Well, I'm going to get even more grumpy," Tommo growled, "if you don't put an end to that **annoying** thing you are doing!"

"All right, then," said Bart, "Just so long as you give me a little smile."

So Tommo looked at Bart. And smiled.

"Still looks grumpy to me," said Bart.

"I have to agree with the big guy," I added.

"Well, I'm doing the best I can," smiled Tommo. Sort of.

"We will have to trust that you are smiling inside," said Bart.

Then we reached Jericho. And there were crowds. And **more** crowds. And crowds behind the crowds.

"What's going on?" asked Tommo. "Is this a special day in Jericho? A feast or something?" And then we heard what the people in the crowd were saying.

"Come to my house, Jesus!"

"Stay with my family, Jesus!"

"Come eat my yummy lamb roast, Jesus!"

"It's us!" I said, amazed. "They're out here because of us. Well, not *us* us. But Jesus and us, obviously."

"Why do they want us to eat with them?" Bart asked. "Not that I am complaining."

"Jesus is famous," explained Tommo. "That's why. And if somebody famous comes to your house than that makes you sort of famous, too."

"I see," Bart nodded. "So my uncle Mezzaliah must have been **very** famous indeed. He was always eating at other people's houses."

"Why did they invite him?" I asked. "What was he famous for?"

"Oh, nobody invited him," said Bart. "He'd sort of just show up around supper time. 'Got any extra grub,' he'd ask. 'I'd be happy to join you.' Mezzie the Moocher. That's what everybody in the village used to call him. I like that word. Moocher. So is 'moocher' the same as 'famous'?"

"No," Tommo sighed. "A moocher is a person who invites himself to eat your food. A famous person is a person who GETS invited."

"Again, you are making so many things clear to me, Tommo," Bart replied. "I bet you are smiling a great big giant smile inside!"

"Sure," Tommo grunted. "Whatever."

"In fact," Bart went on, "you have given me an **amazing** idea. If these people want Jesus and us to come to their house to eat, then we might as well find out what kind of food they make. After all, I would hate to end up at the house of someone who only served turnips. Or any other vegetable, for that matter. Tell Jesus that I will mingle among this multitude and discover who has the **best** grub on offer!"

And before either of us could stop him, off Bart went, diving into the crowd like it was some giant wave.

"I'm not telling Jesus," Tommo grunted.

"Me neither," I replied.

To be fair, though, it looked like Jesus was being kind of picky, too. People would smile and extend their invitation. But then he would smile back and shake his head and **politely** say no. And he did it not once, but over and over again. He did it so many times, in fact, that I wondered if we were ever going to eat.

Then Bart came back. "I did the best I could," he announced, "and here are the results." He cleared his throat. And started tapping his toe . . .

*"There's a woman over there with a twinkling eye
Who wants to make us a chicken pie.
There's a person in the middle called Jochabed
Who bakes thirty-seven kinds of bread.
There's a sculptor in the corner working on that ladder
Who carves his statues out of spleens and bladders.
But the one I like best is some guy named Nick
Whose favourite meal is—"*

"Enough! Enough!" shouted Tommo. "You're doing it again!"

"Goat-on-a-stick," Bart whispered.

"Lighten up, Tommo," I said. "He's just having fun."

"And I didn't even mention your name this time," Bart added. "But I did have an idea:

*'My friend called Tommo would like something fried.
I think that it will make him smile inside!'*

Tommo looked at the floor and shook his head. But before he could say anything, Jesus pointed and said to us, "There he is! That's the man I want to visit!"

Right at the edge of the crowd, there was a fig tree. And, sure enough, up in the tree there sat a man. Well, I say "sat". He was more or less clinging to one branch and shifting about on another. It could not have been very comfortable.

"Why are we eating with a man in a tree?" asked Bart. "Does he live in a tree? Will we have to go in the tree, too? And as for figs, I'm not a fan. Do you think now is the time to tell Jesus about Nick and his goat-on-a-stick?"

"Shush!" I whispered. "I'm sure Jesus knows exactly what he's doing."

But when Jesus said the man's name, I was no longer quite sure.

"Zacchaeus!" called Jesus to the man in the tree. "Zacchaeus, come down. I'm eating at your house today."

And the crowd went **nuts**.

"Zacchaeus?" someone shouted. "Why is he eating with Zacchaeus?"

"The man's a tax collector!" shouted someone else.

"The boss of all the tax collectors!" added another voice.

And then there were too many voices to count.

"He works for our **enemies**, the Romans!"

"He takes more money than he should!"

"He's a bully!"

"He's a cheat!"

"He's a traitor to his people!"

"He's a dirty rotten sinner!"

"No wonder he was hiding in a tree," Tommo grunted.

Then Bart scratched his head. "Hang on, just a minute! Zacchaeus didn't invite Jesus to his house. Jesus invited **himself**! Like my uncle Mezzaliah. So does that make Jesus a moocher?"

"Don't think so," I said. "Look at the guy! He's happy! He's scurrying down those branches like he was some kind of a monkey. In fact, he's not much taller than a monkey. And I thought I was small. No, I think he would have invited Jesus if he could. He was just afraid of how the crowd would react."

"Well, at least we'll be **guaranteed** a good meal," Tommo smiled. An outside smile this time. "Those chief tax collectors are loaded."

"So he's a rich man?" said Bart, scratching his head. "Which could be a problem. Camel-bottom-wise, I mean."

"**Camel-bottom-wise?**" I asked.

"Sure," Bart replied. "Remember that rich guy the other day? He'd done all sorts of good things. Kept the commandments and stuff. And Jesus said that, because he was rich, he was like a camel's bottom that couldn't get through somebody's eye. Or something."

"Like a camel trying to squeeze through the eye of a needle," I corrected him.

"That's it!" Bart grinned. "Well, if that rich guy who did all sorts of good things couldn't make it, what hope is there for this rich guy who has done all sorts of bad things?"

"Jesus told us that anything is possible for God," said Tommo.

And so it proved for Zacchaeus. He was so pleased that Jesus had accepted and welcomed him that he made an announcement to the crowd.

"I'm giving half my money to the poor!" he shouted. "And if I have cheated anyone here, I will pay you back four times more than what I took!"

The crowd was shocked. And amazed. And stunned into silence.

So Jesus took the opportunity to say, "Do you see? You didn't want me to eat with this man. But today, **salvation** has come to him and to his home. He's no

longer a traitor to his people. No, he's a son of Abraham, just like the rest of us!"

Then he waved for us to join him, and off to Zacchaeus's house we went.

"So I guess sometimes camel bottoms do *squeeze* through eyes," said Bart.

"Well, he was willing to do pretty much what that other rich guy wouldn't," I agreed.

"Which means we can look forward to a wonderful slap-up meal!" Tommo grinned.

"And," Bart added, "one last rhyming songy thing to help us on our way:

> *'This is the story of a man called Zacchaeus*
> *Who was little, like a monkey, and climbed up a tree-us.*
> *He was scared of the crowd and just wanted to see us.*
> *And changed his ways 'cause he was welcomed by Jesus!'"*

Chapter 6

HANDS

"What would be the point of saving the jar?"

We were all just sitting around. Resting, really. Jesus and his disciples, getting ready for our next move.

All of us, that is, but Bart, who arrived suddenly with a great big beaming Bart smile on his face.

"You'll never guess what I found!" he announced.

"Oh, I think I can," Tommo grunted. "It's got something to do with food, hasn't it?"

"It does!" Bart grinned.

"Could it have anything to do with goat?" I suggested.

"It could!" Bart's grin grew bigger.

"And a stick, possibly?" sighed Tommo.

"Not a stick . . ." said Bart, mysteriously, pulling something from his overstuffed bag. "A jar! Goat-in-a-jar! **Look**, I got one for each of us!"

With that, he produced three jars filled with pieces of goat.

"Thanks, Big Fella," I said, forcing a smile.

"Yeah," muttered Tommo. "Who wouldn't want a jar stuffed full of unidentifiable goat bits?"

"Exactly!" Bart beamed. "I was going to eat them all myself. But then I thought, no, Tommo and Pip are my friends, and they need to share this unbelievable moment with me!"

"Unbelievable, yeah, that's . . . uh . . . one word to describe it," Tommo grunted.

"But why jars?" I asked.

"It's a new idea," Bart explained. "The man on the stand told me all about it. After you have eaten the lovely goaty bits, you get to keep the jar!"

"A jar reeking of goat grease?" Tommo replied. "Charming."

"You wash it, of course!" Bart replied. "And the next time you want some goat, you just take the jar back and pay them and they fill it up for you. And here's the best bit – they give you money off!"

"Ignoring the fact that I have never seen you wash anything," I said, "what would be the point of saving the jar? There are jars everywhere!"

"Today, yes!" Bart replied. "But as the man told me, who knows what tomorrow will bring? What if we run out of clay? What if we run out of water? And, most important of all, what if we run out of sticks?"

"So there are goat-in-a-jar stands all over the country, then?" I said.

"No, just the one over there," Bart pointed.

"Which means we have to come all the way

back here, to this specific place, if we want to get more goat?" I sighed.

"As the man said," Bart replied, holding his jar in the air. "Re-jarring is not for the faint hearted. It takes commitment. And this jar guarantees that, whatever happens, we will still be able to get goat when we want it!"

"Assuming we do want it," said Tommo, reaching into his jar and pulling out a piece. "What part of a **goat** is this, exactly?"

"It's a question I never ask," Bart replied. "But I have another question. Who is that lady walking over to Jesus with James and John?"

"I think that's their mum," I said. "The wife of Zebedee."

Bart chuckled. "Zebedee. I could say that name all day. **Zebedee**!"

But all Tommo could say was, "Flippin' fisherman."

"Look at that," I said. "She's bowing down in front of Jesus. Now she's holding out her hands, like she's asking for something. Wonder what that's about?"

"Don't know what she could possibly want," Tommo grunted. "Those sons of hers already get all the best jobs. And they get to go off with Jesus

when the rest of us have to stay behind. Well, them and Peter, flippin' fishermen."

"Well, whatever it is," I said, "I don't think they're going to get it this time. Jesus is shaking his head."

"Good!" Tommo muttered. "Maybe one of us will get a look in."

That's when Matthew came running over. "You will never guess what has happened," he said.

"You, too, have discovered goat-in-a-jar?" answered Bart, waving a piece of goat about.

"No," Matthew replied, puzzled. "James and John's mum has just asked Jesus if they could sit on his left and right hand when his kingdom arrives!"

"**Whaaaaat?**" roared Tommo. "Flippin', flippin', **FLIPPIN' FISHERMEN**! I cannot tell you how angry I am!"

"Not as angry as me!" Bart roared along. "This is the most **selfish** thing I have ever heard. If James and John are sitting on Jesus' hands, how is he supposed to eat or change his clothes or blow his nose? How is he supposed to heal the sick or feed the crowds? And not wanting to make assumptions about their hygiene but, if someone sat on your hands long enough, surely their hands would begin to **smell** like your bottom. And how **awful** would that be?"

"Bart," I interrupted but to no avail. The big guy was on a roll.

"And what about goat-in-a-jar?" he went on. "How is Jesus supposed to enjoy the amazing

67

new treat that is goat-in-a-jar? With James on one hand and John on the other, how is he going to even pick up the jar, much less pick out the chunks of goaty **deliciousness** within?"

"Bart," I tried again. "They don't want to sit on his hands, literally. It's an expression, that's all."

"I'll say!" he huffed. "An expression of complete and utter . . . **ummm** . . . concern about what they want and . . . **ummm** . . . not what other people need!"

"That may well also be the case," I nodded. "But 'sitting on the left hand and the right' is something people say, not something they actually do. It means that you are the first and second in command, under the king."

Bart paused for a moment, thinking. "Oh, that's all right then," he smiled.

"It is **NOT** all right!" Tommo fumed. "Those two want to be our bosses, that's what. But they didn't even have the guts to ask Jesus themselves. They had to ask their mummy to do it for them!"

"Well, for what it's worth," said Matthew, "I don't think it worked. Jesus asked them if they could drink the cup he had to drink. They said they could. He said they would. But then he told them that it wasn't up to him to decide who would sit at his right and left hand. It was up to God."

"Hang on!" said Bart. "Now I'm really confused. First we were sitting on hands. But we weren't really sitting on hands. Now we're drinking from cups. So are we really drinking from cups? Or is this another one of those expressions? Or has Jesus possibly discovered goat-in-a-cup? Which would be even more convenient than goat-in-a-jar!"

"I think it's option number two," I replied, "another saying, another expression."

"Which means . . .?" Bart asked.

"Can they go through the things, and experience the hard times, that Jesus will have to go through?" I said.

"Not if they have to rely on their mummy to ask favours for them," grumbled Tommo. "Flippin' fishermen."

"Well, they said that they can," Matthew shrugged. "But who knows? Only time will tell. In the meantime, though, it looks like Jesus is signalling for us to join him."

When he had gathered us all together, Jesus spoke. "Look at the leaders of the countries all around us," he began. "They push their people around. They make a big deal of how important they are. It's all about **power** for them and showing how strong they are.

"Well, I don't want that to be the case with you. If one of you wants to be great, then you need to be the **servant** of the rest. And if you want to be first, then slave away, helping others. Because that's why I came, not to be served, but to become a servant and give my life to set many people free."

"I'm confused, again," whispered Tommo. "Why does he keep talking about dying? The Messiah doesn't die."

"Well, I am not confused at all," Bart whispered back, another great big **beaming** Bart smile on his face. "I know exactly what I am going to do.

I have served my very best friends goat-in-a-jar. And now I shall do the same for Jesus. And I will sit on his hand and drink a cup and be the greatest of all. And I won't even need to ask my mum for help!"

Chapter 7

DONKEY

"Every secret mission needs a lookout!"

*T*ommo and I were on our way to the village. That's when we bumped into Bart.

"Where are you going?" he asked.

"It's . . . uh . . . sort of a secret," said Tommo.

"Ooh, a secret!" Bart smiled. "I love secrets! Tell me. Tell me, please?"

"That's sort of the point of a secret, Bart," I replied. "That you don't tell."

"But I would tell you MY secret!" said Bart. "Go on, ask me. Ask me anything!"

Tommo sighed. "But if we ask you, all you're

going to do is make up another goofy story about one of your goofy relatives."

"Goofy," Bart grinned. "I like that word. Goofy. But this secret is not about one of my relatives. No, it is about the most amazing development ever in the history of portable food."

"But I don't really care about the most amazing development ever in the history of portable food," sighed Tommo.

"You will when you hear this!" said Bart. "It will change your life!"

"It wouldn't, by any chance, have something to do with the greasy bit of rope hanging round your neck?" I enquired.

"It might do," grinned Bart, mysteriously.

"Or the greasy stains on your mouth and fingers?" added Tommo.

"Ooh, you two are clever!" said Bart. "But grease is only part of my secret. The best part, I will admit. But not the whole part, not by a long shot."

"Go on, then," I said. "Tell us your secret."

"Only if you promise to tell me yours," Bart replied.

I looked at Tommo. "I don't suppose it would hurt," I said.

"He'll just keep pestering us till we tell," shrugged Tommo.

"All right, then," I agreed. "It's a deal."

And with that, Bart reached into his Big Bart bag and produced two more greasy ropes with a variety of body parts attached to them.

"Goat-on-a-rope!" he beamed.

Then he handed one to each of us. "Go on!" he grinned. "Put it over your head. Let it dangle round your shoulders. Then take a little nibble every time you feel a bit peckish."

"No way!" Tommo grumbled. "I'm not putting that greasy mess round my neck."

"I'm afraid I would have to agree, Bart," I said. "But it was thoughtful of you to think of us."

"Surely you can see the genius behind it, though," Bart went on. "With the traditional **goat-on-a-stick**, or even the newly developed **goat-in-a-jar**, one hand is always occupied holding the stick or the jar. But with **goat-on-a-rope**, both hands are free! So you can go about your business – fishing, sword fighting, farmering, whatever – and still enjoy the odd goaty treat whenever you want."

"Yes, I can see the advantage," I nodded. "But I still think I'll pass."

"More for me, then!" Bart beamed again, looping both ropes around his neck. "Now, what's YOUR secret?"

"It happened while you were away," Tommo began. "Getting your ropey goat thing, I guess."

"**Goat-on-a-rope**," Bart corrected him. "The branding is very important."

"Anyway," Tommo continued. "Jesus said that he needed two disciples for a very important mission. I figured it was time that somebody got in there before those flippin' fishermen, so I put up my hand straight away."

"Me, too," I added. "Then Jesus took us aside and told us what we needed to do."

"He wants us to go into the next village," Tommo explained. "And find the colt of a donkey. A colt that's tied up and has **never** been ridden. He wants us to untie the colt and take it to him."

"And if anyone asks us what we're doing," I went on, "We're supposed to tell them that 'the Lord needs it.'"

Bart took a bite of goat and rubbed his hands together. "Sounds like a code word!" he said, through a mouthful of meat.

"That's what we thought," Tommo replied. "Like he'd set it all up ahead of time. It was very hush-hush."

"But what does Jesus want with the colt?" asked Bart.

"Dunno," I said. "That's part of the secret, I guess."

"Let's get going, then!" Bart grinned, spitting out a bit of hoof. "I can't wait to see how this turns out!"

"Hang on, Big Fella," Tommo interrupted. "This is our secret mission. Me and Pip. Nobody said anything about you coming along."

Bart's grin turned round into a frown.

"I'm sorry," I added. "But I think Tommo's right. Jesus asked for two volunteers. I don't know what he'd think if three of us showed up with the donkey."

Bart's eyes were looking watery.

"But we do **everything** together!" he pleaded. "We vomit in boats and stay away from leopards and deal with crazy, naked, demon-filled guys. It's always the three of us! So why can't we do this together, too?"

Tommo and I looked at each other. Bart was right, and we knew it.

"Please! Please! Pretty please! With a big slab of goat guts on top!" he begged, tearing off what looked for all the world exactly like a big slab of goat guts from the rope around his neck.

"What if Bart promises to stay out of sight when we give the colt to Jesus?" I suggested.

"Yeah," Tommo sighed. "I guess that would work."

"I know! I know!" Bart shouted, his frown turned round to a smile again. "I can be the lookout! Every secret mission needs a lookout! I'll be way ahead of you. No one will even guess that we're together!"

"Get going, then," Tommo grunted, pointing down the road. "The village is that way."

So off we went, Bart up front and the two of us far behind. It didn't take long to see that we'd made a big mistake.

"LOOK OUT!" Bart shouted, pointing at the road. "Pothole!"

"Thank you, Bart!" I shouted back.

"LOOK OUT!" Bart shouted again, pointing to some shrubbery at the side of the road. "Big jaggery bushy thing!"

"Not strictly necessary!" I called back. But there was no stopping him.

"LOOK OUT, a cloud!"

"LOOK OUT, a rock!"

"LOOK OUT, a scary old fox with crooked teeth!"

And so it went – until the moment he forgot to look out for himself.

"LOOK OUT!" he cried. "A great big steaming pile of . . . oh dear."

"Stepped in it, didn't he?" Tommo grunted.

"Yep," I nodded. "But at least it will keep him quiet for a while."

As it happened, we had already entered the village, and I could see a donkey tied up, ahead of us. We walked quickly past Bart, who was trying to shake the steaming smelly stuff off his foot, and headed straight for the colt. It was tied up right next to its mother donkey, who had her head buried in a feed trough.

So, just as Jesus had asked, we started to untie it. And that's when we heard an unfamiliar voice.

"Why are you untyin' that there colt?"

Followed by a familiar one: "That's exactly what I wanted to know."

"Because the Lord needs it," Tommo replied, smiling at the stranger, then glaring at Bart.

Bart took no notice, of course. "That's a lovely

little colt you've got there," he said to the man, while patting the colt on his head.

"I'm so pleased you think so," the man smiled. "He's my little booty!"

Then he turned to me and Tommo. "I knows that Jesus needs 'im," he said. "But you take care of 'im, mind."

"I'm sure these two strangers, who I have never met before, will do **just** that," Bart replied, winking at us. And that's when the donkey's mum lifted her head out of the trough and turned to face us.

"Yikes!" Bart shouted as the three of us jumped away. "That is by far the ugliest donkey I have ever seen!"

"And the meanest!" her owner chuckled. "There's an old fox around about 'ere she kicked one day. Knocked all 'is teeth sideways, she did."

"Hmmm," Bart mused, "I think I've—"

"Beast!" The owner interrupted. "That's what I calls 'em! Booty and The Beast!"

"That's really interesting," I said. "We probably need to get going, though."

But as I finished untying the colt and went to take it away, Beast gave an almighty snort and sent a hoof flying in my direction. I ducked, narrowly avoiding the old fox's snaggle-toothed fate.

The owner chuckled again. "I might knows that the Lord needs that there colt. You might knows that the Lord needs that there colt. But, by gum, old Beast don't knows it. And that could be a problem."

Then he sniffed the air. And smiled. "Where's that to?" he asked. "That goaty smell?"

"That would be coming from me!" Bart beamed, a finger pointed at his neck. "From a genius takeaway invention called goat-on-a-rope."

The owner inspected the rope carefully. "Impressed, I be very impressed!" he noted. "Liver. 'Orn. Buttocks. And I've no idea 'ow they stuck that clump o' brains on there."

"What did I tell you, Tommo and Pip – or rather, complete and utter strangers?" said Bart. "It's a marvel. A thing of beauty."

"Tha' it is," nodded the owner. "And it just might be the answer to our problems. Turns out that old Beast 'ere was frightened by a goat when she was a young 'un. And it's still the only thing that scares 'er."

Then, with a "Do you mind?" he took the two goats-on-a-rope off Bart's neck and placed them carefully – and very greasily – round ours.

"Don't mind at all," Bart replied. "If I can be of help to a couple of strangers I have never seen before

and will likely never see again, not to mention this Jesus fellow whom I have also never met, then I will consider it a gift well given!"

We finished untying the colt. Beast snorted, then sniffed, then backed away. And off we went, with both Bart and the owner waving us goodbye. Our mission was accomplished, and there were bits of brain staining my tunic and dripping from my hair.

When we finally reached Jesus and the others, Bart was somehow already there.

"An old lady showed me a shortcut," he whispered.

"So what's the colt for?" Tommo asked Jesus. "We figured it was some kind of secret."

"It's actually pretty much the opposite of a secret." Jesus smiled as Peter put his coat, like a blanket, on the colt, and then Jesus hopped on its back. "It's a secret revealed, in fact. You see, there's an old prophecy, from the book of Zechariah, about how God's long-expected king would finally come to his people, riding humbly on the colt of a donkey. People have wondered for some time who I really am. And now it's time to show them."

Then Jesus gave the donkey a nudge, and they started down the hill into Jerusalem.

"Did you hear that?" Tommo said to us. "It just won't be between his disciples anymore. No, now everyone will know that Jesus is the Messiah!"

Then he took off his own coat and threw it on the ground in the donkey's path – a sign of honour and respect for Jesus the king. The rest of us disciples did the same. And it wasn't long before crowds joined us, some laying coats and others laying palm branches on the ground.

Then everyone joined together in a chorus of praise.

"Hosanna to David's Son! Blessed is the king who comes in the name of the Lord! Hosanna!"

Bart, however, felt obliged, for some reason, to resume the role we had given him for our mission.

"LOOK OUT!" he cried. "Those palm branches can be slippy!"

"LOOK OUT! There are some nasty rocks in the road!"

"LOOK OUT! There are some very grumpy Pharisees ahead!"

"LOOK OUT! There is another steaming pile of . . . oh dear."

"LOOK OUT! LOOK OUT! LOOK OUT!"

Chapter 8

TEMPLE

"Somebody ought to do something!"

"So where's Tommo?" asked Bart.

"Up ahead, somewhere," I shrugged. "Talking to Peter, I think. Seems he has another bone to pick with those flippin' fishermen".

"And where are we going again?" asked Bart.

"To the temple," another voice answered.

Bart jumped and glanced at the owner of the voice, and he turned to me and whispered, "Who's that?"

"Thaddeus," I replied.

"Thaddeus?" said Bart, a puzzled look on his face. "Who's Thaddeus?"

"He's one of us. One of Jesus' disciples," I said.

"But why have I never seen him before?" Bart asked.

"You've seen him **hundreds** of times!" I said. "He's been with us for three years."

"Well, I don't remember him," Bart shrugged. "But then I mostly hang out with you and Tommo, don't I? And anyone along the way who happens to be selling goat-on-a-stick. So I guess that makes sense."

"It makes no sense at all," I sighed. "So why don't you just say 'Hi'?"

"Because he's a **Stranger**," Bart replied. "And we don't talk to strangers, do we Pip?"

"Unless they're selling goat-on-a-stick," I muttered. And then I looked over and said, "Hello, Thaddeus."

"Hello, Pip," he answered. "Hello, Bart."

"He's talking to me!" Bart whispered. "What do I say? What do I say?"

"Why not treat him like he's one of your goat-on-a-stick men?" I suggested. "You have no trouble talking to them."

So Bart turned to Thaddeus and said, "I'll have two portions, please. One **extra** crispy. And one with a **double** squirt of goat juice."

Thaddeus smiled. Then he slapped Bart on the back.

"I like your style, my friend," he grinned. "I have always appreciated your jolly jests and japes!"

Bart turned to me, whispering again, "What'd he say?"

"He thinks you're funny, Bart."

"Well, I think he TALKS funny."

"Just say thank you," I suggested. "And maybe say something nice back."

So that's what Bart did. Sort of.

"Thank you, kind sir," he said. "And . . . UMMM . . . I like your hat."

Thaddeus laughed again. "But I'm not wearing a hat."

Bart looked at me. I shook my head.

"Then I like your . . . very nice head of hair . . . piled up on your head that way," said Bart. "Which looks like a hat."

"Very good!" Thaddeus chuckled. "The man says

what he means. I like that. There is no guile in him whatsoever."

"Sometimes there is," Bart replied. "When I have eaten too much goat-on-a-stick."

Thaddeus laughed again. And there was more backslapping, too. And then he announced, "We have arrived! The Temple and its courts stand before us! Erected by Herod the Great over fifty years ago. A beautiful and fitting tribute to our glorious God."

"It's pretty," Bart nodded. "Now let's get into the temple courtyard. I've got some shopping to do!" And off he ran.

For the first time, Thaddeus looked a little perturbed.

"Bart is joking again, surely," he said to me.

But Bart wasn't joking. Not for a minute. The

temple courtyard was filled with stalls where you could buy just about anything. And "just about anything" is what Bart came back with a short time later.

"Look at this!" he beamed. "I bought it from that nice lady over there. She wanted five coins for it, but I knew better."

"I love a bit of haggling!" said Thaddeus. "Fighting, tooth and nail, for that perfect bargain. Holding your ground, beating down the price. So what did you give for it, my friend?"

"SIX coins!" said Bart proudly. "Five was far too cheap."

"But it's just a rock!" Thaddeus observed.

"With a face painted on it!" Bart replied. "A cute, cuddly little face that makes it look just like a rock badger. In fact, she told me that I could make it my own rock badgery little pet."

"But it's a rock, Bart," I said.

"So it will be easier to take care of," he shrugged. "I think I will call it Nigel."

"I'm sorry, Bart," said Thaddeus. "I have to agree with Pip. It's just a bit of cheap tat."

"Don't listen to him, Nigel," Bart whispered to his rock. "Thaddeus doesn't know what he's talking about. And he uses a lot of **funny** words."

"I'm simply trying to warn you, my friend," said Thaddeus. "Shop in the temple courtyard and you are bound to be **cheated**. Take that money changing stall over there, for example."

"You mean the one with the man who looks like a turtle?" Bart asked.

Thaddeus chuckled. "The very one, my friend. And yes, he does resemble the common terrapin. Well spotted."

"I'm not sure he looks like a common . . . turnip . . . but what's wrong with what he's doing?" asked Bart.

"**Everything!**" Thaddeus replied. "If you want to buy an animal to sacrifice in the temple – a dove, say, or a goat – you need to use **special** temple money. So you give that man your regular money, and he exchanges it for **special** temple money. The problem is that every time he does it, he gives you less than he should and keeps the difference for himself. In other words, he takes advantage of the fact that you need the temple money and can't get it anywhere else. And he cheats you."

"But what if you go to one of the other money changers?" I asked. "Do they all cheat?"

"To a greater or lesser extent, yes," said Thaddeus. "Some may not cheat you as much as others, but you will **always** be worse off for using them."

"I did not know that!" I said. "How about you Bart?"

But Bart was talking to his new . . . pet.

"Don't worry, Nigel," he whispered. "I would never think of sacrificing you like a dove or a goat."

Thaddeus smiled. "As it happens, the priests would never accept a rock badger as a sacrifice. Or a rock, for that matter."

"Nigel and I are both relieved," said Bart, tickling his rock under its "chin".

"But if you did want to buy a **proper** sacrifice," Thaddeus went on, "you'd be cheated just the same. Just imagine how hard it is for someone travelling across the country to bring his own animal here."

"Sure," I said. "That's why they sell animals in the temple courtyard, isn't it?"

"At a price far higher than you would pay elsewhere," nodded Thaddeus. "More cheating, more taking advantage of people, especially the poor."

"Somebody **ought** to do something!" I said.

Thaddeus shrugged. "Who, when the temple itself and those who run it benefit from every crooked sale?"

And, just at that moment, Tommo appeared.

"Tommo!" Bart shouted, giving him a big Bart hug. "My friend who talks in words I can understand. And doesn't have hat hair. I have missed you!"

"That's very nice, Bart," Tommo grunted, squeezing out of the big guy's grasp. "But there's something I have to tell you. Jesus is angry. I mean, really, REALLY angry!"

This was news, for sure. Jesus hardly ever got

angry, but when he did, it was usually about something important.

"Let's go!" I shouted, and off we went, following Tommo to where he'd last seen Jesus.

"Hang on, Tommo!" Bart called, lagging behind. "I need to introduce you to my new pet . . . rock . . . Nigel . . ."

By the time we caught up to the rest of the disciples, Jesus didn't just look angry, he was putting that anger to work.

He went over to the tables where they sold the sacrificial doves – and turned over the seats of those who were selling them!

Then he headed for the money-changing tables . . .

"I wouldn't want to be that turtle-headed man," whispered Bart. "Or the man who looks like a common turnip, either."

Moving swiftly, Jesus grabbed the edges of the

money changers' tables and turned them over so that all their coins went rattling and clattering onto the ground! And then he shouted so that everyone could hear, "The Scriptures are clear. 'My temple should be a house of prayer.' But you, you have turned it into a den of **thieves**!"

Thaddeus turned to me. "You reckoned that someone should do something about those cheats," he said.

"And someone has," I nodded.

Then I glanced over to a corner of the courtyard and saw some priests and scribes raising their fists and pointing at Jesus. "But I don't think that lot are too happy about it," I noted.

"Cast your eyes on everyone else, though," said Thaddeus. Nobody is weeping for those cheats, I can assure you. In fact, they all look rather pleased."

"Nigel is smiling," added Bart.

"Nigel is **always** smiling," I replied. "He's painted that way."

"And you would be smiling, too," Bart beamed, "if you had been adopted by someone who loved you and promised to take care of you and would make sure that you would live happily ever after!"

I looked at those religious leaders again, shaking their fists in our direction.

"Happily ever after?" I wondered. "I hope so . . ."

Chapter 9

WIDOW

"Some of those people are giving a lot of money!"

A couple of days later, we were back in the temple courtyard.

"Turtle man is back," said Bart.

"And the dove sellers, too," I nodded.

"Well, you can't expect things to turn around overnight just because Jesus turned over their tables," said Thaddeus.

"Who's that guy again?" Bart whispered.

"For goodness' sake," I muttered. "It's Thaddeus! He was right here with us when Jesus got angry the other day."

"His name's just so hard to remember," said Bart. "Perhaps if I put it into one of my little songs it would help:

"Thaddeus, Thaddeus,
I must remember Thaddeus.
He was here the other day
When Jesus got all Mad-eus."

"Wonderful, Bart!" Thaddeus enthused. "**Imaginative**. Catchy. A work of art. Five stars!"

"Don't encourage him," Tommo grunted.

"**Wait** a minute!" said Bart. "Tommo is here, too? Does that mean there are four of us now?" Then he reached into his bag. "Well, five, to be precise," he grinned, pulling out his pet rock. "Mustn't forget Nigel!"

"I would be **honoured** to be included in your discipling subsection!" Thaddeus beamed.

"What'd he say?" Bart whispered again.

"He'd be happy to join us," I whispered back. And then Bart broke into another one of his "songs":

*"Thaddeus, Thaddeus,
I must remember Thaddeus.
I cannot understand his words,
It makes me kind of sad-eus."*

"Don't be sad, Bart!" Thaddeus replied. "It's a matter of widening your horizons, that's all. Listen carefully to what I have to say and your vocabulary is **bound** to expand exponentially!"

Bart looked at me and whispered, "See?"

"Fair enough," I whispered back. "I didn't get that one either."

And Tommo muttered, under his breath, "Flippin' know-it-all."

"Jesus is waving us over," said Thaddeus. "Maybe we'd better go and see what he wants."

So we joined the other disciples just in time to hear Jesus make a speech. He looked sort of angry again, and he shouted what he had to say so everyone in the temple courtyard could hear. "Watch out for the scribes," he said, "Those religious leaders who try to fool you by the way they look and the things they do in public, for all to see.

"They parade about in their fancy robes. They love it when people recognise their position by greeting them in the marketplace. They get the best seats in the synagogues, of course. And the place of honour at any feast they might attend.

"But it's all show, for when nobody is looking, they cheat widows of their inheritance. And they persuade them to give more than they can afford in the temple offering, impressing them with their long prayers.

"For that," Jesus concluded, "they will be condemned more than anyone else!"

"Wow!" I said, "the religious leaders are already pretty upset with Jesus. They didn't like it when he rode that donkey down the hill."

"And they weren't too happy about what he did to the money changers or the dove sellers, either," said Tommo.

"This will surely make them even more unhappy," said Thaddeus.

"Nigel is unhappy, too," said Bart.

"That's because you turned him upside down," I sighed.

"So I have!" said Bart, turning his rock round the other way. "Thank you Pip, for bringing a smile back to Nigel's face!"

"Don't mention it," I replied.

But Jesus wasn't finished.

"Look over there," he said. "Do you see the rich men putting their money into the offering box?"

We looked. And we did.

"Now listen," Jesus went on. "Listen to the way they send their coins ringing into the box, to show everyone exactly how much they have given."

We listened. And sure enough, we could hear the coins clattering into the box.

"Some of those people are giving a lot of money!" I said.

"Thirty-seven coins, to be precise," Thaddeus smiled. "That's what that man there has given."

"How do you know?" Tommo grunted.

"I counted them, as they made their way down," said Thaddeus. "It's a talent, I have. A gift, if you like. Oh, and listen, that next man is dropping – wait for it – **fifty-three** coins into the box!"

Tommo rolled his eyes, but Bart was overwhelmed.

"That is **amazing**!" he said. "Almost as amazing as the incredible counting feet of my great-uncle Hebadiah."

"Counting feet?" asked Thaddeus.

"Here we go," Tommo muttered.

"Yes!" Bart went on. "Whenever there was a need for counting things in my family, we would always call on Great-Uncle Hebadiah. 'How many sheep are in that field?' someone would want to know. Great-Uncle Hebadiah would look at the field. Great-Uncle Hebadiah would look at his feet. Then he would raise his head dramatically, look at each of us in turn, and say 'ten'.

"Or maybe someone would want to know how many pots were in the workshop. Great-Uncle Hebadiah would look at the pots. Great-Uncle Hebadiah would look at his feet. Then he would raise his head dramatically, look at each of us in turn, and once again, say 'ten'!"

"So did he ever say a number more than ten?" I asked. "**Eleven**, say? Or **twelve**?"

Bart shook his head. "Not that I can recall."

"Or how about a number less than ten?" asked Tommo.

"Only after the accident," Bart replied.

"So is it possible," said Thaddeus, "that your Great-Uncle Hebadiah was giving an answer based simply on the number of toes on his feet?"

"**Dunno**," Bart shrugged, "you'll have to ask him. He was the counting person in the family."

"And speaking of counting," Tommo added, looking suspiciously at Thaddeus. "How do we know you're not just making up the number of coins that those people are dropping in the box. I mean, there's no way for us to check, is there?"

Thaddeus looked offended.

"Really, Tommo?" he said. "Do you honestly think I would attempt to impress you with a clever ruse? What do you take me for?"

"What'd he say?" Bart whispered.

"Do we think he'd try to trick us?" I whispered back.

"No," said Bart, "you would not try to trick us, Thaddeus. In fact, I trust you every bit as much as I trust my Great-Uncle Hebadiah!"

Tommo sniggered. I tried hard not to join in. And all Thaddeus could muster was an **embarrassed** smile and a "Thank you, Bart."

Then Jesus himself put Thaddeus to the test. Well, and the rest of us, as well, to be fair.

"You have heard the coins clattering into the box," he said. "You have seen those rich men trying to impress us with their so-called generosity. But, look, here comes a widow – the victim of their deceit and manipulation. Let's see how much she gives."

We watched and we listened as, one by one, the widow dropped her coins into the box.

"Two," said Thaddeus. "Only two."

"See," said Bart, turning to Tommo. "He really does know how to do it. And he didn't even have to look at his feet!"

"So who gave the most!" asked Jesus.

Thaddeus answered, at once. "The man before the widow!" he announced. "By my count, he dropped sixty-four coins into the box!"

"And by my count," Jesus replied, "you are wrong. Those rich men – all of them – had plenty of coins in their own money boxes, back home. But the widow, the widow gave everything she had. And that is why she gave the most."

Later, as we made our way out of the temple courtyard, Bart leaned over to Thaddeus.

"Cheer up!" he said. "Nobody gets it right every time. Well, apart from my Great-Uncle Hebadiah."

"Thank you, my friend," Thaddeus sighed. "I find a modicum of comfort in that."

"Again, I have no idea what you just said," Bart replied, "but Nigel and I have made up a little song to help us remember this day. It goes like this:

Thaddeus, Thaddeus,
Jesus said to Thaddeus,
"The widow put in most of all
For she gave all she had-eus!"

Thaddeus shook his head and sighed again.

But Tommo chuckled and said, "Bart, I think those songs of yours are finally growing on me. What can I say about this last one? **Imaginative**. Catchy. A work of art. Five stars!"

Chapter 10

NARD

"There are rumours."

"So let me get this straight," grunted Tommo. "We were in Bethany. Then we walked all the way down into Jerusalem. And now we are going all the way back up to Bethany again?"

"That's about right," I said. "But we do get a slap-up meal for our troubles – with Simon the leper."

"I have my introduction all worked out," said Bart, holding out his pet rock: "Nigel, the rock badger, meet Simon the leopard. Two animals at the same dinner. They will get on like a house on fire. Or a burrow. Or a den."

I chuckled. "Apart from the fact that neither of them is actually an animal, why not?"

Tommo, however, was far more blunt. "I don't think that Simon is going to want to meet your stupid rock," he grumbled. "And for the fiftieth time, it's 'leper' not 'leopard'."

"And for the **more** than fiftieth time," Bart replied, "I do not think it is right to refer to people by their disease. That is why I am constantly confused. If you had simply said, 'Simon the person who has leprosy', then there would have been no confusion whatsoever."

"You mean you wouldn't have then thought that Simon owned a leopard?" I said.

"Does he? Really?" Bart beamed. "Then I shall introduce Nigel to Simon's leopard. Perfect!"

"Here's my question," said Tommo. "If this guy is a leper – okay, okay, HAS leprosy – what are we doing hanging out with him? What if we catch it, too?"

"An excellent question, my friend," a familiar voice answered, out of the blue. And the three of us jumped as one.

"Where did he come from?" I wondered out loud.

"He's like a ghost! A know-it-all ghost!" grumbled Tommo.

"Who are we talking about?" asked Bart.

"Hello, Thaddeus," I said.

"Oh, him," Bart sighed. And then he brightened up almost immediately. "Simon has a leopard," he explained. "And we are going to have dinner with the leopard. Or maybe we are going to be the leopard's dinner. Not sure. And I am going to introduce him to Nigel!"

"Ah, Bart, you old jester, you!" laughed Thaddeus, slapping the big guy on the back. "Your random pronouncements are a constant source of entertainment and delight!"

"What'd he say?" Bart whispered.

"He still thinks you're funny," I whispered back. And then I turned to Thaddeus.

"So what's the answer to Tommo's question?" I asked. "Can we catch leprosy from Simon?"

"We wouldn't be going there if we could," Thaddeus replied. "Either he has been cured or he has some other skin condition that looks like leprosy. It is unlikely that he would invite us to his house if we could catch the disease. And even less likely that Jesus would put us in that kind of danger."

"Well, that's a relief," I said.

"But eating dinner with a leopard is also dangerous," mused Bart.

And all Tommo grunted was, "Know-it-all."

"At any rate, here we are!" announced Thaddeus.

"At the house of Simon who has leprosy!" added Bart. "Or something that looks like leprosy. Or a leopard. Let's eat!"

The food looked amazing. And tasted even better. Strangely, however, Bart did not seem to be enjoying it much. In fact, he was hardly eating at all.

"What's up, Big Fella?" I asked.

"Nothing," he muttered, looking under the table and then right round the room.

"There's goat, look!"

"Yes, I saw," he sighed, peering into the next room.

"You're not looking for that leopard, by any chance, are you?" I asked.

"Might be," he muttered. And then he **pointed** at his rock.

"Look at poor Nigel," he said. "He's just sitting there, all by himself. Oh, he puts on that brave smile of his. But inside . . . inside he's crying. I should never have built up his hopes."

"I'm sure he'll get over it," I assured Bart. "He's . . . UMM . . . strong, isn't he? Solid. Difficult to bruise. Built to take life's hard knocks."

"So he is," Bart nodded. "Thank you, Pip. You are a good friend. And it looks like Jesus has a good friend, too!"

While we were talking, a woman had walked up to the table, near to where Jesus was sitting. She had a fancy jar in her hand. And then, without warning, she opened it and poured the contents onto Jesus' hair!

A strong musky smell filled the room, and at the very same time, Bart grabbed his throat and went, "Naaaard! Naaaaaard!"

"Well spotted, my large friend," said Thaddeus. "The woman has indeed anointed Jesus with nard, that most expensive of scents!"

"Noooo," Bart gasped, "Naaard is the sound I make whenever I smell perfume!"

"Then you'd better leave the room, Big Fella!" I shouted.

"I have a better idea!" Bart gasped. And he grabbed a large slice of goat and plastered it on his face. He covered his nose and his mouth. And in no time, he was breathing normally once again.

"Strange cure," noted Tommo.

"Works every time," Bart replied, through a face full of goat. "The smell of the goat covers everything and sends me and my lungs into a happy place."

Gravy splattered everywhere as he spoke – on Bart and on Tommo and on me. So when he turned to Thaddeus, Thaddeus cleverly shushed him and said, "Listen, I think Judas has something to say."

And, boy oh boy, did he!

"That perfume is worth a fortune!" he complained. "And this woman just pours it away.

Surely it would have been better if we had sold it and given the money to the poor."

"He's got a point," I said.

"Nah," Tommo grunted. "Never much liked that guy."

"You never much like anyone!" I replied. "What's wrong with his idea?"

"There are rumours," Tommo muttered. "That's all I can say."

"Well, I am happy to add a bit more," whispered Thaddeus. "As you well know, Judas is the treasurer of our little band of disciples. He keeps track of the coins. And from what I have heard, some of those coins have found their way into his own personal money bag."

"That's bad, really bad!" spluttered Bart, spraying gravy all over Thaddeus.

So you're saying that he didn't want to give the money to the poor?" I asked. "That he wanted to keep it for himself? I think that's a bit of a stretch."

And most of the other disciples agreed, as it happens. They chimed in, one by one, in support of what Judas had said.

But Jesus had an altogether different way of looking at the woman's actions.

"Why are you **criticising** this woman?" he asked. "She has done a beautiful thing for me."

"Or a stinky thing," Bart whispered to me. "Depending on where you're sitting."

"There will always be chances to care for the poor," Jesus went on. "But I'm not always going to be with you. By pouring ointment on me, it's like this woman has prepared my body to be buried."

"Now I'm **really** confused," Bart sputtered.

"We pour oils and perfumes on bodies before we bury them," Thaddeus explained. "It's a way of honouring our dead. That's all Jesus is saying. The woman has honoured him by what she has done."

"And that is why," Jesus concluded, "from now on, when anyone talks about me, this woman will be remembered for what she has done!"

"So is Jesus going to get buried?" asked Bart.

"Not anytime soon, I hope," replied Thaddeus.

"But there was that thing he said to us," I remembered. "The thing about his enemies killing him. Back when Peter said that Jesus was the Messiah."

"Flippin' fisherman," grunted Tommo.

"And there are a lot of people who are **angry** with him, right now," I continued. "Like all those religious leaders we keep running into."

"Well, I don't know about any of that," said Bart, wiping the gravy from his face. "But my slice of goat has run out of 'smell' and I think I'd better leave. **Naaaaard**!"

"I'll come with you, Big Fella," I volunteered.

So out we went, into the street. "I must say," Bart sighed. "I was very disappointed with that feast."

"Well, you had a bad reaction to that perfume," I shrugged. "And you spent most of the meal with goat on your face."

"No, it wasn't that!" said Bart. "I have spent many meals with goat on my face. No, it was the leopard. I never got to see the leopard."

"Bart," I said, "Would you be terribly bothered if I told you that there never was a leopard?"

"I don't know," said Bart. "Would you be terribly

bothered if I told you that I just saw Judas sneak out onto the other end of the street?"

"Where?" I asked.

"Over there!" He pointed. "I think we should follow him."

"Why?" I said.

"So we can be spies again!" Bart beamed. "Like when we found the donkey." And before I could answer, off he went, tiptoeing after Judas.

He looked ridiculous. Of course he did. He tried to hide behind a tree. He tried to hide behind a bush, he tried to hide behind a dog. But Bart was so big that nothing could hide him. Give him his due, though, he did manage to stay well behind Judas, who never spotted him, not once.

And then Judas turned a corner, and Bart turned to me with a finger on his lips. I crept up behind my big friend. We both stuck our heads around the corner.

Judas was talking with someone. And not just any someone. No, he was talking with priests and scribes!

We couldn't hear what they were saying, but the jingle-jangle of coins changing hands was more than clear.

"Why is Judas giving them money?" Bart whispered.

"I don't think he is," I whispered back. "I think they gave the money to him. And a lot, by the sounds of it. Look, here he comes, and there's a bulging bag in his hands!"

We hid in the shadow of a doorway. And fortunately, when Judas reached the corner, he set off in the other direction.

"Should we tell somebody?" asked Bart, when Judas disappeared down the street.

"Tell them what?" I replied. "That our treasurer is taking money from scribes and priests? Maybe we're wrong. Maybe they like us more than we think. Maybe they want to help."

"Or maybe Tommo and Thaddeus are right," said Bart. "And Judas is up to something not very nice."

"Maybe," I nodded. "I guess time will tell."

"I can tell you one thing," said Bart, looking at his pet rock, "Nigel is Not very happy. Secret meetings in the dark. He has his suspicions, he does."

And even though I wasn't ready to admit it, I had my suspicions too.

Chapter 11

HANKIE

"The prophetic hankie never fails!"

Tommo was grumbling again. As usual.

"Flippin' fishermen."

"What have they done now?" I asked.

"Just gone and taken the best job we ever had," he muttered.

"Running a goat-on-a-stick stand?" said Bart. "That is annoying."

"We have never run a goat-on-a-stick stand," I was quick to point out.

"It's still annoying," Bart shrugged.

"Except that they are not running a goat-on-a-stick stand," Tommo grumbled. "Jesus has sent Peter and John off on one of those secret missions. You know, like when we found the donkey?"

"And its incredibly nasty mum," Bart shuddered.

"Maybe it's for the best then," I said. "That was one scary donkey."

"That's Not the point!" Tommo shouted. "WE were the "Secret Mission Guys"! And now they've gone and taken that, too. Flippin' fishermen!"

"Why don't we follow them?" Bart suggested. "And secretly join them on their secret mission. I'm a good tracker!"

"You did manage to stay out of sight when you followed Judas the other night," I nodded, "I'll give you that. But it's daytime now. Surely that's harder."

"Not if, like me, you have been trained by one of the **great** trackers of our time: Nahum the Nostril of Nazareth!"

Tommo rolled his eyes.

"I don't think that another story about one of your relatives is going to make Tommo feel aNy better," I suggested.

"But Nahum the Nostril of Nazareth was not one of my relatives!" Bart insisted. "He was a family friend, sadly departed now, and renowned for his ability to sniff out the location of anyone or anything!"

"So he trained you to do the same thing, right?" sighed Tommo. "Which means you probably have some awful nostril-based story to tell us. I think we already know where this is going."

"Which is my point, exactly!" Bart beamed. "Due to his incredibly sensitive sense of smell, Nahum could sniff out both where someone had been and also where they were going!"

"That's impossible, Bart," I argued. "I mean, it makes sense that he could work out where someone had been because of the scent on their clothes, maybe. But how could he smell where they were going?"

"With his amazing prophetic hankie!" Bart replied. Then he reached into his bag and produced the most disgusting piece of cloth I had ever seen.

"Please don't say that you're going to let that thing touch your face." Tommo gagged.

"It is a **sacrifice** I am willing to make," said Bart solemnly, "in the memory of Nahum the Nostril and for the sake of my friends."

Then he placed the hankie over his nose and blew. The cloth fluttered more or less in a slightly-to-the-left direction.

"They went tHataway!" Bart announced.

Tommo sighed again. "Of course they did. You can see them walking away. Look!"

"Proof, once again, that the prophetic hankie never fails!" Bart grinned. "Let's go!"

And so we followed after Peter and John.

"I still don't get how your hankie is going to help us stay out of sight," I said.

"Unless it can also **magically** grow into a giant sheet." Tommo grunted. "And even then, I'm not going anywhere near it!"

"Grow into a giant sheet?" Bart sniffed. "That's just silly."

"And a prophetic hankie isn't?" Tommo moaned.

"No," Bart went on. "The hankie will allow us to

lose sight of them completely and then find them again. You'll see."

"I don't know," I said. "I think we have a really good chance of losing them all together that way."

"Trust the **hankie**!" said Bart, waving the disgusting thing about. And that's when Peter and John turned a corner. "No worries!" Bart said. And he put the hankie to his nose and blew. "The hankie says they went left!" he announced.

"Yes!" Tommo shouted. "We just watched them turn left!"

But Bart had already left us behind and turned left round that corner, too.

"No, wait, Bart!" I called. "They'll see you!"

But when Tommo and I turned that corner, too, they were nowhere to be found. Not Peter. Not John. Not Bart and his **magical** hankie, either.

"Where'd they go?" said Tommo, looking round.

"They couldn't have gone far," I replied.

"So what do we do now?" Tommo asked.

"Wait, I guess," I suggested.

So we went back round the corner and, every

now and then, stuck our heads round to see if we could see them.

After a while, Bart came out of one of the houses, whistling a happy little tune.

"Where have you been?" Tommo shouted.

"On a **secret mission**!" Bart beamed. "In an upstairs room!"

"I know I'm going to regret this," Tommo replied, "but explain!"

"It's really very simple," said Bart. "After my prophetic **hankie** led me around this corner—"

"Where we had already seen Peter and John go," I interrupted.

"The hankie led me straight to them," Bart went on. "As a matter of fact, they were standing right round the corner talking to a man with a jar, and I nearly knocked them all down!"

"So what did they do?" asked Tommo. "Did they tell you off? Flippin' fishermen."

"No, they were fine," said Bart. "They didn't seem to mind that I was there. They followed the jar man into a house and he took them to his upstairs room. So I went along, too. It was a very nice room, as it happens. Quiet. Out of the way. I was especially impressed with the tasteful decor. There was an amazingly long table in the middle that, for some reason, only had seats down one side."

"So what was it all about?" I asked. "Why were they there?"

"Oh, to prepare the Passover meal," Bart explained, "for us all to eat later. That's what Peter and John are doing now."

"And they didn't want your help, I suppose," Tommo grumbled. "So they sent you away. Too important a job for the likes of us. Flippin' fishermen!"

Bart shook his head. "No, it wasn't like that, at all. They asked me to help, but I explained to them that, while I was very good at eating, I wasn't that good at making things TO eat. Apart from goat-based meals, that is. And seeing as there is no goat, or goat juice, or goat fat, or goat drippings in your **average** Passover meal, there wasn't much I could do. At that point, I pulled out my hankie – not for prophetic purposes, but simply to blow my nose – and, for some reason, they were very happy to let me go."

"No surprises, there," Tommo grunted.

Later that day, we went with Jesus and the rest of the disciples back down the same street and into that upstairs room.

"I brought my hankie in case Peter and John couldn't remember the way," Bart whispered to me.

I wanted to laugh, but it didn't seem appropriate. Jesus looked really sad.

"I have something to tell you," he said. "And hard as it may be to believe, it's the truth: one of you is going to betray me."

Now everybody round that table looked sad.

"Is it me?" Bart whispered, tears in his big Bart eyes.

It seemed ridiculous. "No," I whispered back. "Of course not."

But he wasn't the only one asking that question. Everyone seemed to be afraid that maybe they had done something, or were about to do something, that would betray our friend and our teacher – the one we had followed faithfully for three years.

"That's right," Jesus went on. "One who has shared this meal with me, who has dipped his hand in this dish with me, will be the one to betray me."

Now Bart was even more upset. "I'm sharing the meal with him!" he sniffled. "I dipped my hand in the dish! Look, I even got a little sauce on my sleeve!"

"We all ate from that dish!" Tommo chimed in. "That's the point! It's one of us, one of his own disciples, who is going to betray him – whatever that means!"

"I have to suffer, as I have said," Jesus went on, "I have to leave you. But woe to the one who betrays me and makes that happen. It would be better for him if he had never been born."

That's when Judas looked at Jesus. Looked him right in the eye. "It's me, isn't it, teacher?" he asked. And his expression was a strange mixture of sadness and guilt, like somebody who'd been caught stealing from someone he loved.

"You've said it," Jesus replied.

I nudged Bart, who was trying hard to wipe the **splodgy** bit of sauce from his sleeve.

"The other night? When we followed Judas? Remember? He wasn't taking money from those priests to help us. He was taking it to betray Jesus!"

"So it wasn't me, then?" Bart sighed. "Thank goodness. This stain is not coming out."

Amazingly, we carried on with the meal. I'm not sure anybody really felt like eating. I know I didn't.

But then, as if things hadn't been strange enough, Jesus took some bread and thanked God for it. Then he broke it into pieces and passed it round to us. "Eat this," he said. "It's my body."

I looked at Bart and Tommo. They looked at me. None of us knew what to make of it.

"What's he mean?" Tommo whispered. "How is this bread his body?"

But everyone else was eating it, so we did too.

Then Jesus took a cup of wine. He thanked God for that as well. "Drink this," he said. "It's my blood. For when it is poured out, my blood will bring **forgiveness** and bring us all into a new relationship with God."

So we drank, but poor Tommo looked more sad and confused than ever. "None of this makes any sense," he whispered. "Blood poured out? If Jesus is the Messiah, he's not supposed to have his blood poured out. He's supposed to **win**!"

But there was nothing happening that night that looked like Jesus was about to win anything.

When the meal was finished, we sang a song of praise to God and walked to the Mount of Olives.

"In one way or another," Jesus said. "You are all going to leave me tonight. It's like the Scriptures say, 'I strike the shepherd and the sheep scatter.' But when I am raised, we will all gather together again in Galilee."

We lingered at the back, as usual, and Tommo just kept shaking his head. "What's happening here?" he muttered. "Scattered? **Struck**? Raised? What is Jesus going on about?"

Then Peter spoke up. "Even if everyone else falls away," he said, "I will never leave you."

"There he goes again," Tommo grunted. "Flippin' fisherman."

"No, Peter," Jesus sighed. "Tonight, before the cock crows to welcome the morning, you will deny that you even know me. Not once, not twice, but **three** times."

"That put him in his place," Tommo whispered.

But it didn't. Not at all. "I'll die before I deny you!" he said.

And what could the rest of us do but echo those words after him?

At last we came to a place called Gethsemane, and Jesus told the rest of us to wait while he took Peter and James and John off to pray with him.

"You don't need to say it," I whispered to Tommo. And he didn't. He just sat there with his head in his hands.

Bart was pretty subdued, too. "I am so confused," he sighed. "Body and blood and bread and sheep. I don't get any of this. And I'm kind of scared. Usually it seems like Jesus can handle anything. Storms and leopards and naked demon-filled guys. But tonight he just looks tired and sad, like he wants to give up."

It looked that way to me, too. And when, after a long wait, Jesus and the flippin' fishermen **finally** returned to us, it looked even more that way. Jesus had been crying. You could see. And Peter and James and John were rubbing their eyes, like all they wanted was a good night's sleep.

Sadly, that was the last thing that was likely to happen, for suddenly, without warning, men with torches and clubs and swords descended on us from out of nowhere!

We all jumped to our feet, terrified. And Bart, bless him, put his big Bart self in front of me and Tommo to protect us.

Then out from that crowd came Judas. He walked right up to Jesus. "Hello, teacher," he said. Then he kissed Jesus on the cheek. Like he was his friend.

But it wasn't friendly at all. It was a sign, so the men would know who to arrest.

"He's a rat! A dirty stinking rat!" Bart grumbled.

Peter, true to his word, did even more than that. As the men grabbed hold of Jesus, he grabbed a sword and started waving it about. But he was a fisherman, after all, not a soldier. And all he managed to do was cut off one poor man's ear.

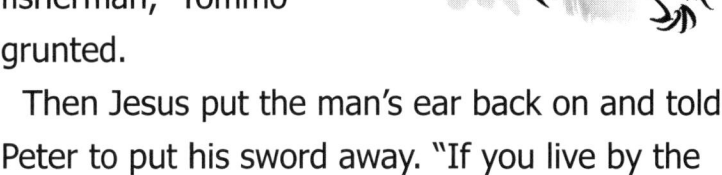

"Flippin' sword-swingin' fisherman," Tommo grunted.

Then Jesus put the man's ear back on and told Peter to put his sword away. "If you live by the sword, you'll die by it, too," he said. "And besides, don't you think that, if I wanted to, I could ask my Father in heaven for help and he would send twelve legions of angels to rescue me? No, I have to go with these men so that **everything** that Scripture says about me will happen."

So he did. He went with those men, a prisoner.

And the rest of us? We did just what he said we would do. We scattered, like frightened sheep, and ran for our lives.

Chapter 12

GHOST

"Nobody has seen Tommo."

The door was locked. It had been locked for three days. We were hiding. Hiding and hoping that the people who had put our friend Jesus to death would not find us and kill us, too.

We were all there – Jesus' disciples. Well, all but two of us. Judas was missing, of course. But nobody had seen Tommo either.

"Do you think he's all right?" Bart asked me.

"Dunno," I said. Because I didn't. The last time I'd seen him, we were all running from the garden, trying to get away from the men who were arresting Jesus. And Tommo was shaking his head and shouting "This is **not** right! This is not supposed to happen. Not to God's Messiah." And then he disappeared into the darkness.

"Do you think we should try to find him?" Bart asked.

"Not until we know it's safe," I replied. "And I have no idea when that is going to happen."

"But we can't sit here forever!" said Bart.

"An **excellent** observation, my friend," came another voice.

"Who's that?" Bart whispered to me.

"For goodness' sake," I answered. "It's Thaddeus!"

"Oh, him," Bart sighed.

"I realise that you are devastated both by the loss of Jesus and the disappearance of the third part of your little triumvirate," said Thaddeus. "Rest assured, we are all grieving with you."

"What'd he say?" Bart whispered again.

"He knows you miss Jesus and Tommo," I interpreted. "And the rest of us do, too."

Bart forced a little smile. "That's nice."

Then he pulled his pet rock badger from his pouch. "Look," he said. "It made Nigel smile, too."

But Nigel and Bart were pretty much the only ones smiling in that room. John was the lone disciple who had been there to see Jesus die on the cross, and a few of the other disciples were across the room, quizzing him again about exactly what had happened.

Bart rolled Nigel around in his hands for a moment. And then tears started rolling down his cheek. "I just wish everyone would stop talking about it, that's all," he sniffled. "They did horrible things to hurt Jesus. Then they killed him. Why can't we leave it at that?"

"People deal with their sorrow in different ways," explained Thaddeus. "Sometimes going over what happened helps."

"Well it doesn't help me," Bart whimpered, shoving a finger into each ear. And then he just started saying "Shut up. Shut up. Shut up." Until it turned into a shout, "SHUT UP!"

That's when somebody banged on the door. And everyone did, indeed, shut up.

"It's us! Let us in!" It was Mary and some of the other women from our group. And when Peter unlocked the door, they rushed in, breathless and excited, their words tumbling out together.

"It's empty—"

"Jesus' tomb is empty!"

"The stone was rolled away!"

"We saw angels—"

"They said Jesus is alive!"

Thaddeus rolled his eyes and turned to me. "Preposterous!" he said. And he wasn't the only one saying it.

"Wishful thinking," he went on. "That's all it is. Women can get very emotional about this sort of thing. Carried away by whimsy and so forth."

"Hang on!" replied Bart, who had removed his fingers from his ears by this time. "My mum was a woman, and she was no emotional mimsy or whatever it is you just said. She was dependable and level-headed and had a mole on her forehead that looked like a camel."

"Yes, well, not meaning to cast aspersions on your mum," Thaddeus said, "but women are simply more likely to be caught up in flights of fancy than men."

"Well, I think you're the one who is full of cat persons and flying fancies!" Bart huffed. "Mary and Joanna and . . . and . . . Other Mary have travelled with us for a long time, and some of them even pay for the grub we eat. So I think we can trust them to tell us the truth. And, for your information, Mister Smarty Pants, Nigel does, too!"

"Well, Peter and John must think there's something to it as well," I interrupted. "They just said that they're going to the tomb to check it out. And, yeah, I know what Tommo would say."

Bart wiped a tear from his eye. "Flippin' fishermen," he sighed. And it sounded almost beautiful.

It took a while, but when Peter and John came back, they were as excited as the women had been. And a little confused, too.

The stone that covered the entrance to the tomb had, indeed, been rolled away. The tomb was empty. Jesus' graveclothes were folded up neatly. And he was nowhere to be found.

"I'm quite certain there *is* a logical explanation for all of this," said Thaddeus. "Perhaps the Romans removed the body. Or the religious leaders."

"But why?" I said. "What would be the point? It was the Romans who put the guards there in the first place, wasn't it?"

"I'm with Mary and Other Mary and those angels," said Bart. "If they say that Jesus is alive, then he's alive. And I'm just looking forward to seeing him again!"

We weren't the only ones having this discussion, of course. As the day went by, every one of Jesus' disciples and friends tried to **puzzle** the thing out.

To be fair, it was far better than what we had been doing for the last three days. Better than crying. Better than despair. Better than waiting in dread for that knock on the door. There was **hope** now – even if it still seemed kind of impossible.

Then there was a knock on the door! And when the door was opened, Bart leaped to his feet and shouted, "Look! It's our friends! Cleopas! And Mrs Cleopas! They have a lovely little house down the road, in Emmaus. They are both great walkers. And Mrs Cleopas makes the most amazing goat and goat-gut pie!"

Then he rushed across the room and gave them a Big Bart bear hug.

"Something amazing has happened!" they tried to say, their voices muffled by Big Bart's big belly. And when they finally pulled themselves free, their words tumbled out in the same way the women's voices had, earlier in the day.

"We were walking home to Emmaus—"

"A stranger joined us."

"We told him what had happened to Jesus."

"He taught us from the Scriptures."

"We got home—"

"We invited him in to eat with us—"

"And when he broke the bread, we knew who it was!"

"It was Jesus! He's alive!"

Bart raised his hand. "Was it goat and goat-gut pie you were going to feed him?"

"Not now, Bart!" I said. "Who cares about the pie? The point is that Jesus is alive!"

"Yes, and we already knew that," Bart replied. "The ladies told us, hours ago! I think it's high time we moved on to pie."

And then Jesus appeared in the room.

"See," said Bart, matter-of-factly. "There he is!" But there was nothing matter-of-fact about it.

The door was locked. He hadn't **knocked**. He just showed up, right there among us, like a ghost. And that's what most of the people in that room thought Jesus was.

So some of them screamed. And most of them trembled. Except for one person, of course. He walked right up to Jesus. "Everybody thought you were a ghost the night you walked on the water," Bart said to Jesus. "But I **knew** it was you. And I know it's you now."

Then Jesus looked at the rest of us and said, "Why are you frightened? Why do you doubt that it's really me? Look at the nail prints in my hands and in my feet. Touch them, go on. Ghosts don't have bones. But I do."

Bart wasn't afraid. Not for a second. "I'm so sorry they hurt you," he said to Jesus. "It still makes me want to cry."

Then he touched Jesus' hands and turned to us with a Big Bart smile. "Not a ghost. It's him! It's really him!"

While the rest of us shook our heads, shocked, or raised our hands to praise God, Jesus made a simple request. "Does anyone have anything that I could eat?"

Bart looked expectantly at Mrs Cleopas. "I'm sorry, Bart," she said, "I didn't bring any goat and goat-gut pie with me. But there's a bit of fish on that table over there."

So Jesus ate the fish. Not something your

average ghost would do. And when he had wiped the fish crumbs from his mouth, Jesus sat us down and showed us, from the Scriptures, that the Messiah was always meant to suffer and die and then come back to life again.

He'd said it a lot, I know, one way or the other, but we just didn't want to see it. Or believe it. But now it all made sense.

He also told us that we were meant to go to every nation and tell them what we had seen and that they could be **forgiven** by God through what he had done.

Then, just as he'd appeared, he was gone! And, wouldn't you know it, that's when Tommo finally showed up.

Bart grabbed him and hugged him so tight that I thought Tommo's head was going to pop off.

"You will not **believe** what has happened!" Bart beamed. And, sadly, Tommo didn't.

We told him everything we had seen that day. We explained that we had got it all wrong – that the Messiah was supposed to die and come back to life. And that he wanted everyone in the whole world, not just our own people, to follow him and return to God.

But Tommo just kept shaking his head. "I'll have to see it for myself," he grunted, "Put my fingers in the nail prints. Put my hand in the hole in his side. Otherwise, I won't believe it and that's that."

As the days went by, we tried to talk to Tommo again, but he wouldn't have it.

"**C'mon**, Tommo," Bart pleaded. "We're all happy and Jesus-is-alive-again joyful, and you're still moping around like he's dead."

"You are kind of bringing the rest of us down," I added.

"A party pooper, so to speak," said Bart. "Though no one is accusing you of actually pooping. Just acting like you've had a poop. At a party, I guess. It's a strange saying."

"It's not a 'saying', at all!" Tommo moaned. "It's just another crazy thing you've made up. Like magical hankies and mudbeards and bizarre relatives. All of which I was willing to put up with. But when you pretend that our best friend has come back from the dead, well that's one crazy, made-up thing too far!"

Bart looked really sad. And hurt. So I rushed to his defence. "But it's not just Bart this time!" I said. "We were all here. We all saw him! Me. Thaddeus. Peter. James. John."

But all Tommo did was mutter "Flippin' fishermen" and turn and walk away.

A few more days went by, and both Bart and I had pretty much given up trying to convince our friend.

But Jesus hadn't. And while we were all gathered together in that **locked** room, he showed up again! "Greetings, lads!" he said. And then he looked right at Tommo and held out his hands.

"Put your finger in the nail prints," he said. "Go on. It's all right. I understand. Or put your hand in my side, if you'd rather. Just believe. That's all that I'm asking. Believe that it's really me."

Tommo looked at me. He looked at Bart. He looked **amazed** and filled with wonder, like the very first day we met him. Back when Jesus turned water into wine.

"You-know-who really is the you-know-what," Bart

said. "That's what you told us all along, Tommo. And you were right."

And then, without putting his hand or his finger anywhere, Tommo fell to his knees before Jesus.

"My Lord and my God," he whispered.

And we were all together, again!
Later that day, when Jesus had disappeared again, we were sitting around, laughing and talking.

"So what now?" asked Tommo. "Do we carry on following Jesus? I don't know about you two, but I think it's gonna be a little tricky appearing with him in locked rooms."

"Dunno," I shrugged. "There was that thing he said about us telling the world what we had seen. Maybe he wants us to split up and do that."

"I hope the three of us can do it together," said Bart. "I would hate to be split up from you two.

And I don't mind where we go, so long as it is a place with cakes. And goats, of course."

"I sort of like the idea," Tommo grunted. "No flippin' fishermen for a change. Just the three of us together, wandering the world, telling people about the adventures we had with Jesus.

"Feeding that enormous crowd," I smiled.

"Goat-on-a-stick," said Bart.

"Naked demon-filled guys," remembered Tommo.

"Goat-on-a-stick," said Bart.

"My friend Mary coming back to life again," I added.

"Goat-on-a-stick," said Bart.

"Making friends with a tax collector," grinned Tommo. "And before you say '**goat-on-a-stick**' one more time, Bart, surely there was more to our adventures than that!"

"Of course," Bart replied. "There was goat-on-a-rope. And goat-in-a-jar." And as if in response, his tummy growled. "Don't know about you two," he said. "But I'm feeling a little **peckish**. Like Jesus, I am not a ghost. I am flesh and bones and I need to be fed!"

That's when Mrs Cleopas emerged from the next room with a steaming hot treat.

"I don't believe it!" Bart beamed, "A goat and goat-gut pie!" Then he chuckled. "And Tommo won't believe it either, unless he sticks his finger in it!"

Tommo rolled his eyes. "Am I going to have to put up with this **forever**?" he sighed.

"Dunno," Bart shrugged. "But Not-Quite-Believing-What-His-Very-Best-Friends-Said-About-Jesus-Being-Alive Tommo does have a ring to it."

"Well, I believe it now," he said.

"And that's all that matters," I replied.

"All that matters?" said Bart. "Surely not. There's **plenty** of time for that other stuff. All that matters when one of Mrs Cleopas's delectable dishes is sat before you is to dig in and gobble it up before it gets cold. So come on, lads," he concluded, cutting three large slices, "Let's have some goat and goat-gut pie!"

Hanging Out with Jesus

Adventures with my best mates

Bob Hartman

Big Bart, Tommo and me, Pip. Three guys on a three-year adventure, hanging out with Jesus, finding out what he's up to. Not exactly the best known of the twelve disciples, but we're on the edge of the action – out of the limelight, where there is plenty of partying, messing about and time to make idiots of ourselves.

We're best mates. And Jesus' mates, too. Every day with Jesus is so special, I've written the stories down; stories you'll find in the Bible if you take a look. Well, sort of, because everything is just a little bit different when you're hanging out with us.

978-1-78893-029-1

BibleForce

The first heroes Bible

Do you know the true heroes of the Bible?

Dive into the action and adventure of the Bible! *BibleForce* retells the Scriptures using stunning art and a fast-paced narrative that children can understand. Following the events of the Bible in chronological order, the simple, straight-forward retelling of the scripture will keep children totally captivated. You and your child can read about Bible heroes together, and the text is simple enough for young ones to read on their own.

BibleForce includes over 150 of the most epic stories in the Bible, retold in a dramatic art style which brings characters to life. Hero profiles for key characters help children deepen their understanding and maps and a timeline help set the scene for the stories.

978-1-78893-004-8

God's Amazing Plan Bible

The price he paid to win your love

Amy Parker

God's Amazing Plan Bible seeks to emphasise the ways God works to bring about salvation; from choosing His people and saving them from slavery to establishing them as a nation and finally, at the right time, sending His Son Jesus Christ, the ultimate saviour.

Each story ends with key Bible verses for the reader to reflect on. These verses, taken as a whole, are like beads on a string, connecting the Bible storybook to the biblical text while also connecting the reader to the main message, theme, or idea of each story, expressed in the Bible's own words.

With easy to read language and engaging colour illustrations, this is perfect for 8-12 year olds to understanding the overall themes of the Bible.

978-1-78893-110-6

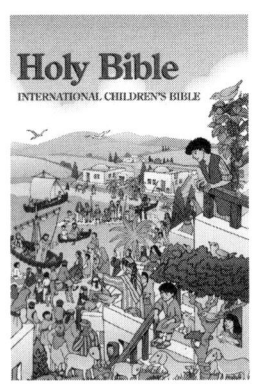

International Children's Bible

The *International Children's Bible (ICB)* is not an adult Bible especially packaged for children. It has specifically been translated directly from the Hebrew and Greek texts into English so that it can be read and understood by children between the ages of 6 and 12.

The *ICB* is a full text Bible that every child will be delighted to own. With guidance, daily Bible reading can easily become a pleasurable habit that will last a lifetime.

Features include:
- Large, easy to read type in two columns
- Simple footnotes explain names, customs and phrases
- 32 full colour illustrations with multi-cultural images
- A dictionary explains difficult words and phrases
- Presentation page
- Colour maps
- Ribbon marker

With simpler language and extra notes and helps, the *ICB* is the perfect Bible for a child who is ready to move on from a picture Bible to a full text Bible.

978-0-85009-901-0

My Diary: Emily Owen

Emily Owen

Emily Owen was an energetic teenager who loved music – and life. But dreams of becoming a teacher, enjoying music and sport all crashed when she was given the shocking news that she had NF2, a genetic condition that had caused tumours in her brain, which would lead to deafness.

Emily's life would be completely different from the one she had planned. She had to let go of the life she had hoped to live – but what could she do? She chose to live a life wholly focused on God.

Written as diary entries, children can see first-hand how Emily learnt to trust God in all her circumstances. Real, raw and honest but ultimately inspiring, Emily's story demonstrates that, even though life might not work out as expected, God has a plan – and there are still everyday rainbows to be found.

978-1-778893-166-3

Authentic

We trust you enjoyed reading this book from Authentic. If you want to be informed of any new titles from this author and other releases you can sign up to the Authentic newsletter by scanning below:

Online:
authenticmedia.co.uk

Follow us: